D0047272

TEA LEAVES
Devotional Meditations for Women

Compiled by Nancy Stutzman

Written by twelve missionary mothers—see
biographical sketches on pages 345-350

Illustrated by Anne Miller, Ruth Yoder, and Margaret Beachy
Cover Photo: Christian Light Publications, Inc.

Christian Light Publications, Inc.
Harrisonburg, VA 22801

**Dedicated
to our
supportive husbands:**

**David Stutzman
David Herschberger
Delbert Birky
Eli Glick
Ervin Barkman
Jason Bontrager
John Weaver
Melvin Glick
Nolan Byler
Samuel Nisly
Vernon Martin
Verton Miller**

Acknowledgements

I owe gratitude to:

David, my husband. He had faith in my vision—enough faith to lend his listening ear for many hours, to offer his gentle criticism, and to provide his financial support.

Regina, my daughter. Without her help in the daily household duties, my task would have been impossible.

Anne, who wouldn't let my dream die once it was born, who proofread enthusiastically.

Rosy and Martha for lifting up my weary hands again and again by offering encouragement and suggestions.

My mother and others through whose prayers we were greatly aided in our writing.

The Compiler

PREFACE

Several years ago, in southern Belize a few of us missionary sisters were having struggles. I was suffering sorrow because of the death of my son. Another sister was plagued by emotional stress and another faced physical problems.

We had two-meter radios for business communication, and the Lord directed us to begin a time of spiritual communication and call it "Tea Time." This five- or ten-minute period each day when we five mothers took turns sharing prayer burdens, verses, poems, and thoughts that were meaningful to us was a time of much encouragement. Much of what was shared we wanted for later reference, so we began writing out our "tea" for the benefit of each other. Soon our pages were enjoyed by a wider circle of friends.

Women everywhere share basically the same conflicts though their settings are different. *Wouldn't there be other mothers who would be open and ready to encourage others by their experiences?* I wondered. There were. These mothers responded willingly, yet were humbly aware that their pens were only tools in God's hand. They have exposed their lives and homes to you. Even as they were writing these meditations, some passed through sickness, pregnancy, adjustments to another culture, and the keen piercings of death. Daily they labored under their responsibilities as wives and mothers. Because ten of us left our home country to share Jesus Christ with other peoples, there is a distinctly foreign flavor pervading the meditations. However, the same spiritual battles are reflected in the writings of the two missionaries at "home."

We hope this book will bring you encouragement, edification, and comfort, even as we have been rewarded in writing.

Nancy Stutzman, Compiler

v

CONTENTS

INTRODUCTION

Tea Leaves is a devotional book for women. As you read the "leaves" of this volume, you will observe that women everywhere have much in common.

The dozen missionary and ministers' wives who submitted these pages do not claim to be professional writers. Yet they have a message to convey. Through their trials and their triumphs, their faith in God has been refined and enlarged. This they want to share with others.

While those in mission settings may identify most readily with the illustrations in these pages, women in all walks of life will understand the responses to circumstances depicted here.

The Editors

CHAPTER ONE

*"My Spirit Hath Rejoiced
in God My Saviour"*
Luke 1:47

1

Lord, I Come to You

READ: John 6:65-69

"Lord, I come to You," and my heart is comforted
already, just in coming.
"Lord,"
    my Saviour,
    the Lord of my life, who knows, understands, and
        plans all for good,
    the One who has all the power I need for this hour.
"I come,"
    so needy,
        in my weakness and my inability,
        with burdens pressing on my heart,
        when my tongue cannot frame the words or utter
            my deep longings,
        with tears of sorrow for my wretched failures, and
            needing your forgiveness.
"To You"
    in trust, claiming Your promises,
    in confidence, acknowledging that You know what
        You are doing in my life,
    for comfort in the cares that fret and wear,
    for strength to plod on faithfully and know this too
        shall pass.
"Lord, I Come to You," with gratitude that You are
    there.

Delighted

READ: Psalms 36:5, 6; 37:4, 11; 40:8

"Delight thyself also in the Lord . . ."
Lord,
I will delight myself
  in You.
I am delighted
  with Your boundless supply of love.
I am thrilled
  with Your patience.
I am glad
  for the privilege
  of being Your daughter.
Your faithfulness
  reaches the clouds (so high!).
Your righteousness
  is like the great mountains.
Your judgments
  are a mighty deep.
I am delighted, Lord,
  for the privilege
  of knowing You
  personally.

I am delighted
  with the abundance of peace.
Peace—release
  from friction
  between me and another.
Release
  from tension,
  from burdens,
  from physical illness.

3

Peace with myself
   (who and what I am is good
   because God made me that way).
Peace with my husband
   (especially after we've disagreed).
Peace with my child.
Peace with brothers and sisters
   in the church.
Peace with You
   through the blood
   of Jesus.
I am delighted, Lord,
   with the abundance
   of peace
You've given me.

I am delighted
   with doing
   Your will.
Your will—
   a story for my little child
      or a time to hold and listen,
   a pitcher of Kool-Aid
      for my husband,
   a request for help
      with sewing a dress,
   a drink for a traveler
      passing by,
   an enforced rest
      through illness,
   a stubborn vehicle
      or one out of gas
      or one with a weak battery
      or no vehicle.
I am delighted
   with doing
   Your will, Lord.

4

(I'll have to confess, Lord, I haven't always been delighted. But I am willing to be.)

I will delight
    in Your commandments, Lord.
You ask me
    to love,
    to forgive,
    to persevere,
    to grow,
    to be kind,
    to give,
    to rejoice.
Lord, I am delighted
    with Your commandments.
Aid me, Lord,
    in doing them.

". . . and He shall give thee the desires of thine heart."
My desire:
    to love Thee more deeply
    and to love my fellowmen generously,
    without prerequisites.
My desire:
    a pure heart,
    untarnished attitudes,
    sincere and upright motives.
My desire, Lord:
    a closer, more intimate walk with You.
This, I know, You have promised.
And I am delighted!

Computers

READ: Psalm 139

Computers amaze me.

Computers can keep track of sales, customer payments, and stock in warehouses. They can figure out employees' wages and print their paychecks.

Then I read . . .

"Thou knowest my downsitting and mine uprising, thou understandest my thought afar off. Thou compassest my path and my lying down, and art acquainted with all my ways. For there is not a word in my tongue, but, lo, O Lord, thou knowest it altogether. Thou hast beset me behind and before, and laid thine hand upon me."

Computers can control machines that make bread, chemicals, steel products, and paper.

Then I read . . .

"For thou hast possessed my reins; thou hast covered me in my mother's womb. . . . My substance was not hid from thee, when I was made in secret, and curiously wrought in the lowest parts of the earth. Thine eyes did see my substance, yet being unperfect."

Astronauts use computers to keep their spaceships on course. Engineers use computers to check the designs on buildings and bridges and dams.

Then I read . . .

"In thy book all my members were written, which in continuance were fashioned, when as yet there was none of them."

Lord, how marvelous are *Thy* works. Thy thoughts cannot be numbered, no, not even by a computer. Computers, after all, can only put out what man puts into them.

God's Five Senses

God hears: READ: Psalm 145:19
    my songs of praise and joy,
    my desperate whisper, "Lord, I can't take
      anymore,"
    my words of biting sarcasm.

God sees: READ: Psalm 33:18
    how full my day has been,
    how weak and tired I am physically,
    the needs of those He sends me to minister to,
    when my baby falls (He said He sees the
      sparrow's fall),
    all the little irritations and faults of others
      that He allows in my experience.

God smells: READ: Genesis 8:21
    the sacrifices—the yielding of my will,
            the giving of my precious
                things willingly and gladly.
    His Word says this smells sweet to Him.

God tasted: READ: Hebrews 2:9
    God the Son tasted death for me.

God touches: READ: I Samuel 10:26
    hearts—my heart with compassion (Lord,
          touch my heart again), sinners'
          hearts with repentance (Thank You,
          Lord, for Eugenio's confession on

Sunday), brothers' and sisters' hearts, moving them to help each other (I'm so glad Nancy is coming to help me this afternoon).

And God feels: READ: Hebrews 4:15
   the weight of our responsibilities,
   the burden of our physical limitations,
   the personal grief we feel for others'
      problems.
"Behold, the Lord's hand is not shortened, that it cannot save; neither his ear heavy, that it cannot hear" (Isaiah 59:1).

Calling In

READ: II Timothy 1:7-14

God,
   Your daughter calling again,
      ringing in on II Timothy 1:7.
Take away the spirit of fear:
   fear of our unknown future—
      where? when? what from here?
   fear of people not liking me.
   fear of rejection,
      of disappointments,
      of smashed dreams.
And replace it with Your power:
   power to keep the victory.
   power to be a Proverbs 31 woman,
      a pleasing wife,
      and a patient mother—today.
   power to maintain a cheerful spirit
      to all doorcallers
      (as if it were Jesus at my door).
   power to show kindness to children
      who call or come to play.
—and Your love:
   love for Your Word
      and You.
   love for Your precious gift to me—my husband.
   love for Your blessings to us—our children.

love for myself—(Instead of condemnation)
   for I was Your idea.
love for the unlovely.
love for my brothers and sisters in Christ.
love for the souls of all men.
—and a sound mind:
  a sound mind when I feel frazzled
    and worn every whit;
  a sound mind when my emotions are screaming
    at the seams for release;
  a sound mind when I've had "too much"—
    too much of exposure,
    too much of people,
    too much of demands,
    too much of pressure.
God, I need You today:
  with all of my weary being,
   I lift my tired hands
  and reach out to accept,
  not fear,
    but power
      and love
        and a sound mind.

Prayer of a Missionary Mother

READ: I Corinthians 1:3-9

Thank You, God, for many things
    that come our way—
Those daily interruptions,
    the knocking at our door,
So many things we hadn't planned for today!

Thank You, God, for the people who need us—
    just to lend some bread
    or to share the concerns and burdens on their
      hearts.
Give us patience, Lord; forgive us when we fuss!

Thank You, God, for our home—
    may it be a palace of love for our children,
    a haven of peace for my husband,
    a shelter for those who roam!
Thank You, God, for friends who pray—
    interceding in our behalf,
    their kind letters of encouragement
    making it possible for us to stay!
Thank You, God, thank You!
    for what You have done in the past
    and for what You are doing now
    and for your continual care in the future, too—
      Father, we thank You!

Thank You

READ: Psalm 111

Thank You for hibiscus flowers
  and a little girl to pick them
  and a little boy to bring me a whole peanut butter
    bucket full.
Thank You for a daddy
  who likes to work with his son
  and took time this afternoon to share his work with
    Nathan.
Thank You for a daughter
  who, when asked if she wanted to do dishes or start
    laundry, said, "You do what is easiest for you,
    Mama."
And after camping for a week, thank you for
  running water,
  bright lights at night,
  a washing machine,
  a sink where I can wash dishes without stooping,
  good detergent,
  sweet-smelling pillows,
  . . . and teatime!
Thank You for Anne—
  her energy and enthusiasm lift the heart.
Thank You for Rosy—
  her thankfulness and lack of complaints lift the
    spirit.

13

Thank You for Martha—
    her dedication to the Lord, her husband, and her
        children lift the evaluation of my work to a
        higher plane.
Thank You for Judy—
    her quiet submission to all circumstances lifts my
        desire to fulfill my highest mission.
WHAT A RICH WOMAN I AM!

Bucketsful of Blessings

READ: Psalms 68:19; 107:9; Proverbs 10:6; 28:20

Raindrops by the millions,
    by the bucketsful,
    —oh, ever delicious.
Mother Earth lifts up her empty cup
    for filling.
The occupants of Mother Earth
    lift up their empty hands
    to the Source
    and all say,
    "Thank You."
Thunder, lightning
    in the dark hours . . .
Wee frightened voices from the next room,
    "Mama! Daddy!"
The response, "Come, let's cuddle."
    Family beds are made for such nights!
Then we listen to the music
    of beautiful rainfall
    and we sleep!
My heavenly Father sends blessings, too,
    by the bucketsful.
I stretch my thirsty being to SEE them—
    a hug from my husband,
    a flower from my daughter,
    a "you look good in that dress"
        from a sister,
    Creole bread from the policeman's wife,

15

a good book,
an encouraging letter,
a radio contact,
a Scripture verse,
an afternoon of rest and relaxation,
an uninterrupted night of sleep.
I stretch again to RECEIVE the blessings
and say, "Thank You, Father.
I appreciate them."
Then the lightning and the thunder times—
I hear Him calling during those dark hours,
"Come over to Me. I'll cuddle you and hold you
tight till the storm's over."
Dark times are made for such as this.
Then together we listen to His music
and I can rest and fall asleep . . .
I am loved.

Future Worries

READ: Luke 12:22-32

Lord, I've so many fears and doubts
    About the future days.
It seems I can't accept them
    Just by faith, in Your own ways.

I wonder very anxiously
    When placed 'neath pressures strong,
Whether I can hold together
    And endure the whole day long.

And supposing when the pressures come,
    I'll feel weak—as today—
Never thinking of the strength You shower
    Upon me when I pray;

Or how You've undertaken
    In the past—in days gone by—
When I've trusted You for courage
    An "impossible" to try.

Please forgive me, Lord, I pray Thee.
    I need courage for today,
Not for future tests and trials,
    Which may never come my way.

Take these anxious cares far from me.
Help my trust to be complete.
Take this heavy load I carry.
Lord, I lay it at Your feet.

I don't want to borrow worries
Which may never come at all.
Thank You, Lord—for rest abideth.
I know You'll answer every call.

In our times, we usually aren't faced with the uncertainty of where our next meal will come from. We do not worry if there will be warm clothing for the coming winter months.

But our anxieties may be about things just as crucial.

Let us thank God that we cannot see our future path, but we can know the One who holds the future.

Petitioning

READ: John 14:13-18

Her day begins before the sun rises.
The angels silently looking on
  see her by her sacred spot
    with her face to the ground,
    her lips moving.
She seeks the Highest.
Another day—
  strength, Lord . . .
    to wash the dishes and clothes,
    to cook the meals (what for dinner today, Lord?),
    to sweep and tidy the house,
    to clean dirty bodies and wipe runny noses,
    and change messy dresses again and again.
Another day—
  patience, tenderness, Lord . . .
    to listen to children's questions and endless chatter,
    to read them the same books over and over,
    to reassure them and love them and touch them,
    to be their friend and play with them,
    to deal fairly in discipline,
    to let them help knead bread or wipe the floor
      or lick the cake bowl.
Another day—
  emotional stability, Lord . . .
    to accept interruptions as ministries,
    to maintain a cheerful and welcome spirit to
      doorcallers,

19

to find reassurance from You that I'm normal
    when I'm lonely or when I cry
    or when I miss my friends
    or when I've had "too much."
Another day—
    love, Lord . . .
        for the chocolate-skinned youngsters
            who walk in uninvited and begin to explore,
        for the mothers who come to talk
            and others who come to watch.
Another day—
    Grace, Lord . . .
        to be pleasing to my husband today,
        to do him good and not evil,
        to be loyal, supportive, and loving,
        to live in a "glass house,"
        to accept gracefully our lack of privacy
            and lack of normal living,
        to lay down again my rights and what I want
            on the altar
            and say "Yes, Lord" to Your will, what You want,
            when, and however long You want,
        and then, Lord, grace to see You in all of today
            and to see all that comes to me today as from
                You.
    So be it.
The form rises.
    She pledges . . . her utmost for His highest.
        The angels carry her requests,
            and the Father answers . . .
                . . . she is a mother.

The Secret Place

READ: Psalm 90:1-4

There is one room in my house for which I have great appreciation. It has served me well in both trouble and triumph. This room is my meeting place with God.

The "Prayer Room" is located at the quietest end of the house. It is tiny but does have a desk, chair, and cot. The clock, posters, and bookshelf along with the shaded window provide an atmosphere conducive to meditation.

This is my place of safety, my place of refuge, my "hiding place." Here I can tell God everything. I can leave feeling refreshed, restored, renewed, ready to face more storms and more battles. Here I find comfort, assurance, and promises from God's Word.

This is my meeting place with God.

He Gently Leads
Those With Young

READ: Isaiah 40:1, 9-11

"Every Christian must have a daily quiet time. The early morning hours are best. If you don't have your devotions, your whole day will go wrong."

So we've been told, and what mother of preschoolers has not felt guilty and frustrated at her failure to carry this out consistently?

How can you get up early if you've been up many times during the night, and now everyone is still sleeping and you would like to do so too? Or you do decide to get up before the rest, only to have the baby wake up, too.

I remember having three preschoolers and deciding that right after breakfast I would have my devotions before I started the day's work. This meant, however, that I didn't get at my housework or laundry (no automatic washer!) until well into the morning. And I was frustrated! So I decided to have it after lunch while the children napped, and I found peace in my decision.

At another stage in our family's life, I did try the early morning schedule again and it worked. Many times one of the children would get up during this time too and come and quietly snuggle up to me and look at a book. Or if I was already praying, the child would kneel beside me as I put my arm around him until I was finished. He sensed it was a special time.

I'm glad God understands mothers with small children and knows their need and desire to spend time with Him. He is aware of those days that just don't seem to have a block of time when this is possible and every attempt at it is interrupted. Even on those days He can penetrate through your consciousness and whisper His peace and remind you of a promise. As you go from one task to another, the tender Shepherd will "gently lead those that are with young" (Isaiah 40:11d) in green pastures of communion with Him.

Meditation

READ: Psalm 119:1-24

As we sat in the livingroom one evening, each one occupied with his own activity, our eight-year-old asked, "Mom, what is meditation?" She was memorizing Psalm 119 as a school assignment. I tried to explain how it is letting God's Word be digested in our souls—really thinking about the words and how they fit us personally, just as our food is digested and gives strength throughout our body.

She went on studying, but I was still thinking about meditation. David's meditation was on *His* precepts. So often "things" crowd out my meditation.

We need to spend time alone with God each day. But since many of our duties don't take a conscious effort, we can meditate while we are doing dishes, mending, sweeping floors, or hanging out laundry. If we simply let our mind wander, it often makes plans for the future, and we forget we are strangers here, as verse 19 says. If we allow it to, our mind will remember the ill-treatment we received from someone, nursing a grudge so as not to let it die. In verse 14, the writer compares God's testimonies to great riches. How often do I let my mind think of the earthly possessions that are a little too dear to me, or some I wish I could have!

I want the meditations of my heart to be such as would give strength to my soul. I want them to penetrate my being to the extent that when an unforeseen trial threatens, my faith will cling to *His* precepts.

24

Rest Found in Waiting

READ: Isaiah 40:12-31

She came to my door, looking for someone to share her lonely hours. I had much to do for my family. Secretly, I hoped she would hurry on. Must I give time to this lady while my needs keep growing?

The phone broke through the quietness of the afternoon. I was terribly tired from the midnight hours spent with a teething baby. Someone needed a listening ear, a heart to share the burden she was bearing.

I made plans for great accomplishments today, only to have them ruined by irritating interruptions, slicing my day into little bits and pieces.

"Lord, my strength is gone. Where is Your promise of renewed strength? I'm weary. Nothing goes the way I plan. I don't even have time to provide for my family's needs. What am I doing wrong?"

God asks, "My daughter, what have you given? You've given time—to whom does time belong? You've given your plans—who makes your plans? You've given your strength—I can renew it once again. You need rest more than you need sleep—rest is found only in yielding yourself to *My* control. Do you recall what I have given for you?"

"O Lord," I cry, with penitential tears. "I've given naught. Forgive me. Take my all. Such peace, such strength floods my soul. The weariness has fled and *You* are in control."

At Every Turn of the Road

READ: Psalm 24

"Blessed are the pure in heart: for they shall see God" (Matthew 5:8). After we get to heaven? Yes. But also in the here and now. I love to hear people testify to seeing God in some unexpected circumstance or even in just an everyday experience. Yes, He is there, at every turn of the road, waiting to show Himself and His ways to His children. And when our hearts are pure, free from bitterness and anger, we can see Him.

We are told that the first man to orbit the earth said he didn't see God out there, and therefore concluded that God didn't exist. Several years later another astronaut was so awed by the experience of seeing Earth from space that he read Genesis 1:1 while in orbit and "saw" God all around him.

When Joseph's brothers sold him as a slave to Ishmaelite merchants, Joseph could say, "Ye thought evil against me; but God meant it unto good" (Genesis 50:20). His heart was pure, and he saw God in his circumstances.

A young missionary, eager to get on with witnessing and discipling was asked to scrub and wax floors in preparation for a Bible study group. Such activity was not very challenging! But she was able to see God's hand in the arrangement and the value of balance in

26

doing physical labor, too, when one has constant contact with people.

One morning the Lord reminded me of wrong and unloving attitudes I had toward a certain family. I confessed my sin, and He cleansed me and filled me with His love for them. That very afternoon the husband came to our bookstore, and through his purchases, I discovered they were having difficult family problems. I was able to give encouragement and promised to pray for them. God's timing was perfect, and I recognized His hand in preparing my heart.

Keep your hands clean and your heart pure, and it will be exciting to "see God" throughout your day!

Take Time to Be Holy

READ: Psalm 1

My mother asks wistfully, "When are you going to visit with me?"

Friends say, "Come early and stay all day. We've hardly seen you since you're back."

My mother-in-law reminds me, "You haven't been at my house much. Come more often."

My sister wails, "Your furlough is almost over, and we've hardly been with you."

The church sings in perfect four-part harmony, "Take time to be holy./Speak oft with thy Lord."

My heart cries, "How, Lord? How can I take time to be holy on furlough? How can I spend time in prayer and Bible study when loved ones are so eager to be with us?"

We need time alone with God. Our souls become parched without Him. But how, on furlough, does one get away from people?

The home folks mean it so well. They show us love by inviting us to meals. The fellowship is rich; so is the food. It's wonderful to be with friends and relatives again. But what about time with God?

When I'm on furlough, I need to remind myself that God is my best Friend. He's my dearest Relative. Why should I give Him crumbs of leftover time after giving prime time to other friends and relatives?

Heavenly Father, I want to keep my priorities in order. I resolve to take time to be holy, even on furlough.

A Small Answer to Prayer

READ: Psalm 119:65-72

We usually think of flies being bothersome and a real nuisance. Early one morning, though, I was thrilled to have a bothersome fly visit me.

You see, in the weeks before this particular morning, I had been struggling in my prayer life. It was so easy to slide along without meaningful prayer. The Lord graciously brought me to the end of myself and to a recommitment in this area. I didn't know how this particular morning's quiet time would go since I was behind in sleep due to a busy schedule. I sleepily knelt in prayer . . . Then the Lord sent the fly!

"Lord, are there other answers to prayer I have missed?"

God Provides for Us

READ: Psalm 121

When we left Guatemala and returned to the U.S., we had no idea what the Lord had in store for us. We didn't have much money to live on, so we were trusting God to care for our needs. Vernon was looking for a job as a farmer, so it wasn't quite as simple as finding work and then a house. He was looking for a place to live and work in the same package. Thus, it took some time and careful consideration.

We were home one week and had not found a definite place when someone we had not seen for some time came up to me and handed me an envelope with our name on the outside. He told me that someone had asked him to give it to us.

In private we opened the envelope, not knowing what to expect, and were shocked to find $700 with a note from an anonymous brother. He felt God leading to share this money with us. What a definite answer to prayer! God provided over and above that which we even dreamed.

"I will lift up mine eyes unto the hills, from whence cometh my help. My help cometh from the Lord!"

What Shall I Pray for Next?

READ: Matthew 7:7-11

Sometimes I feel God takes a special delight in answering prayers, especially those of new Christians. He knows just what it takes to make Himself real and to stimulate faith.

I listened intently to a dear sister as she related answers to specific prayers. Her life hadn't been easy, and by the time she was a young teenager, both her parents had died. Her childhood alternated between boarding schools in the winter and life on the Indian reserves in the summer, where she saw much drinking and immorality. So her first prayer was that someday she would have a "sober" home. Today that is a reality.

After several years of marriage and no children, she said she asked God for a child as Hannah did (I Samuel 1:11), and they did have a son. As the child grew, she wanted to send him to a Christian school, but finances were a problem. So she prayed again, and today he is attending the Christian school.

She and her husband had been Christians for some time but were not yet baptized due to some obstacles. She decided to pray about it in a specific way, and in a short time we witnessed the happy occasion when they took this step together. Her next prayer concern came from the conviction that they should tithe their income. Soon after this they attended a family seminar and her husband was also led to understand that they should begin systematic giving.

"Now I'm wondering what I should pray for next," she said in a gentle voice as a smile crossed her face. Just then her son came from school and together they left. But these examples of her childlike faith in our loving heavenly Father made a deep impression on me. I was challenged also to trust Him Who said, "Ask, and ye shall receive, that your joy may be full" (John 16:24).

He Understands!

READ: Psalm 25:10-22

It was Saturday morning and I felt overwhelmed by all the things waiting to be done. My husband and I were to leave for a week of meetings, and there were many details that needed to be worked out at home for the time of our absence. On top of this we were to have visitors for supper. In my desperation I dropped to my knees and told the Lord I really didn't want to entertain visitors that evening. (You might as well be honest with the Lord. He knows anyway!)

Imagine my amazement when just a few minutes later, the phone rang and our visitors called to say they wouldn't be able to make it for supper! I could hardly believe my ears! I had expected the Lord to answer by giving me the willingness and the strength to carry me through. Instead, He chose to give me just what I desired. So again I bowed and my heart overflowed with humility and thanksgiving to my precious Lord who cares and understands all about me. The goodness and thoughtfulness of God melted my spirit in reverent worship.

Sometimes God deals with us in sternness or gives us grace to go through with difficult obligations. Other times He honors our honest confessions and deep cries of human weakness and gives just what we ask. Either one can bring the desired results of obedience and worship.

33

Complaints and Conclusions

READ: Matthew 14:22-26

People—
  people—
    and more people.
I sigh.
  They make me so tired,
    till I want to see no more.
Stenciled pineapples on my cupboard doors?
  I know. Hospitality reminders.
    Scriptural commands to be cheerful?
  I know better there too.

Father,
  I'm only baring my soul—
    being honest.
  You love me anyway. I know.
    Of that I am certain.
  And You understand. Even Your Son
    tired of crowds
      and hid Himself after a long, weary day
        of constant inquiries.
Even He needed a break and an occasional
  retreat for refreshment.
So I conclude I'm normal.

34

And anyway, isn't admission of my need
and where I am now (my feelings)
the first step to healing?
So—You know my need
and my inner heart desire
to be cheerful,
happy,
to love these people,
to accept interruptions as ministries.
I'm putting out an S.O.S.
and believing You
to supply all my needs
as You promised.
You are able
and BIG ENOUGH.
"Thank You, Lord."

(Written after a morning of 45 doorcallers!)

Conviction and Continuing

READ: Matthew 14:27-33

People—
  people—
    and more people.
You heard me last week, God.
  Was I complaining?
    Maybe.
You brought conviction.
  I repent of my selfish spirit,
    of not wanting to be bothered,
    of wanting to be left alone.
Thank You for showing me that
  without people
    we would have no ministry,
    no fulfillment.
  For working with living material
    is the most fulfilling ministry
    (sometimes the most frustrating too).
Perhaps You meant it that way
  so we lean the harder,
    and trust You more.
So I thank You
  for being my Master Teacher
  and for continuing this course
    in Your school
  and not considering me a
    dropout.
I need growth.
  You will give it.

How God Works

READ: Colossians 1:9-12; Hebrews 13:20, 21

One day I knelt by my bed and prayed, "Oh, Lord, I am Your child. I am giving myself to You completely. Work in me what You want to work. Make me what You want me to be. Bring me back to a closer, more intimate relationship with Jesus as my Best Friend."

In the days that followed I reaffirmed my commitment to God. I reminded Him, "I'm Yours, Lord. Work in my life."

And then, God took away my husband. Oh, not completely. Just now and then. My husband had to be gone evenings—lots of evenings, it seemed. When he was home, he was often very tired—too tired to enjoy an evening of companionship.

And people came and filled up his *days* with requests for his help. No time to work on projects we had hoped to complete before rainy season set in. No time to do things I wanted done around the house.

I rebelled. I felt sorry for myself. I blamed my husband. I complained. I said to myself, "I will be a martyr."

Then I began to look, really look, at what God was doing. He was answering my prayer. He was working in me (at least He wanted me to let Him!). He was making me what He wanted me to be. He was bringing me back to a closer, more intimate relationship with Jesus my Best Friend.

Once again I prayed, "Oh Lord, I am Your child. Keep on working."

"I know that, whatsoever God doeth, it shall be for ever" (Ecclesiastes 3:14).

37

Gaining Through Losing

READ: Matthew 10:37-42

We grow up in a culture where winning or gain is the ultimate. From childhood we have played games to win. We have been taught to work hard, to make a living, and at the same time to make gain or extra. We have believed that gain or success is fulfillment. But God's principle is gain through loss. Whoever will lose his life shall find it, and whosoever decides to save his life is going to lose it!

The humanist says YOU are important. Seek your own pleasure. Look out for yourself. You deserve happiness, ease, riches—you work for it; it's yours! But Jesus says lose yourself (take the emphasis off you), and become involved in others. Be willing to give up your own comforts, your own interests for My sake!

Learn the "So That's" God has planned for us!

We become weak *so that* we might experience His strength. Sickness and physical problems teach us to depend on Him and give us a longing for heaven, for new bodies!

We experience tribulation *so that* we may know how to comfort others. How often we have experienced suffering, bereavement, and other trials, only

38

to meet someone else who is going through a similar trial, and we can reach out to them because we understand!

We leave Father and Mother, brothers and sisters, our home and land, for the sake of the Gospel *so that* God can give us many others who become as dear to us as our own family!

We experience poverty *so that* we can experience the true riches laid up for us in heaven.

We find ourselves broken and empty *so that* God can fill us with HIMSELF!

39

God Cares When I Hurt

READ: Psalm 103:1-14

My baby has caught one of these terrible tropical bugs. (Or did it catch her?) She's hospitalized because of dehydration. The needle keeps slipping out of her tiny veins, and the intravenous feeding has to be restarted many times. I ache to hold her but can't because her arms and legs are tied.

Poor baby! She's hoarse from crying. Bewildered, her eyes search mine. She can't understand what's happening.

"Why doesn't Mama hold me?" she seems to be asking. "Why does she let these strangers hurt me? Doesn't she care?"

If only she knew how much I do care. It hurts me to see her suffer. But I can only stroke her, pray, sing to her, and cry with her.

Sometimes I'm like my baby. I hurt and I wonder if God doesn't care. I can't understand what's happening nor why my heavenly Father allows it.

But God does care. "Like as a father pitieth his children, so the Lord pitieth them that fear him" (Psalm 103:13). He knows why He allows the things that happen to me. Painful experiences help me grow, make me a better person. Through it all my Father is with me. And He cares when I hurt.

40

Martyrdom

READ: Psalm 31

I will never forget John's death. Shot. Killed. A missionary of the Gospel. I thought God protects us if we are in His will. And here I had been sleeping amidst gunshots, screams, dogs barking at night, death squads who suspected foreigners, guerrillas who despised the religious. Visions of the angel of the Lord encamping round about us had given me peaceful slumber.

That death changed my life. We evacuated our mission post. I never returned to work there.

That death changed my heart. I became suspicious of a God who calls a person to serve, then allows his death when He has all power to prevent it.

For months I lived in mental blackness. When I read the Old Testament, I'd think, *Couldn't God find better ways to deal with man?* When I was admonished to trust God, I was sure He was tricking me into my deathtrap. When I saw a bitter patient in the hospital, I wondered if divine healing wouldn't bring that person to salvation quicker than suffering would.

The carnal mind is enmity against God. It is too awful to remember more of the blindingly black reasonings my "intelligent" mind invented. I was

41

drowning in unanswerable questions. I needed help. To whom could I turn? To God.

God, I commit myself to You—Your plan, whether I understand it or not, whether the world sneers or scolds. *(Why do You live so far from civilization?)*

I commit myself to trust You. Though You slay me, yet will I trust You. I will follow the mission dream You put in my heart long ago, even if it leads to my death or the death of the one I love.

I have asked You all my questions and have found no answers, only blackness, terror, despair. It is hard on my pride that my reasoning mind cannot understand. Here dies self, reason, pride, doubt.

I tremble to make this commitment. I tremble more at the blackness within if I withhold it. God I give You my life, *and my death*, for Your glory. Amen.

Modern Psychology or God?

READ: Psalm 63

O my God,

Let me not wonder if I love myself sufficiently. Rather let me wonder at the love You have shown to me. To me, a person of little importance.

Let me not search out whether I have an inferiority complex. Rather let me search with all my heart for You, who are "meek and lowly in heart."

Let me not seek a good self-image. Rather let me seek You, who made Yourself as nothing. Who did humble Yourself further unto death. You, whose only image of Yourself rested on the Father's good pleasure in You.

Let me not pursue my ministry. Let me pursue You, who came to minister and offer Your life to ransom me.

My daughter,

"Ask, and it shall be given you; seek, and ye shall find; knock, and it shall be opened unto you" (Luke 11:9).

43

Emotional Health

READ: Psalm 86

Dear God,
Why did You create woman's physiology to be so vulnerable to up-and-down emotions? It humbles me. I thought I was strong emotionally, stable mentally. Now I realize mental health is a gift from You, not my strength of character or ability to cope.

The days I have to beseech You to keep me from falling apart make me more thankful for the days You give that gift without my asking.

That I must worship You in spirit and truth has troubled me. How can I know my worship is spiritual and not just emotional? But those days that are stripped of glad feelings, when I am committed nonetheless to obey Your command to rejoice, I know my worship is not merely emotional. It must be in spirit. There is nothing else to cling to then.

Humble. Dependent. Thankful. Prayerful. Worship in Spirit. God, is that why?

Invisible Blessings

READ: Psalm 56

With a peace my heart's o'erflowing—
  Peace the world can't understand.
I have a few of earth's possessions.
  I'm a stranger in the land.

No, they can't see why happiness
  Should all my being thrill.
But I have some hid possessions
  God has shared, my life to fill.

He gave peace and joy, contentment
  When He took away my sin.
Cleansed me by His precious Son's blood.
  Guilt's all gone. He lives within.

They know not why I am singing
  While the mighty billows roll.
They can't see I'm safe with Jesus.
  He's the anchor of my soul.

They can't see the hand I'm holding,
  Which belongs to God in heaven.
Nor the Shepherd who is leading,
  Though the journey's all uneven.

I thank You, God above me,
  For the peace the world can't give,
And for constantly abiding
  By my side while here I live.

As I endeavor to train my children these few short years they are with me, I want to concentrate on teaching them that the invisible blessings which God has so abundantly given us are those which can never be taken away if we cling to them in faith. May they have the kind of faith which sees and knows the invisible better than the visible.

I Will Trust

READ: Isaiah 12

Our family was visiting at a remote Indian village. We didn't burn any oil and the night was dark. Our five-year-old daughter just couldn't sleep. She was afraid and started crying. Her whimpering didn't help my inner qualms at all!

Finally in desperation we asked her to say, "I will trust and not be afraid." Over and over Daddy asked her to repeat the same words. "I will trust and not be afraid. . . . I will trust and not be afraid. . . . I will trust and not be afraid."

Soon she stopped crying and went to sleep. The comforting words of Scripture once again had brought peace to troubled minds—not only to hers, but mine as well.

Never Alone

READ: Matthew 28:16-20

The neurologist finished examining my husband, then sat at his desk and told us what we feared.

"You're losing the function of your leg. If you don't want to become a cripple, you'll have to have your disk removed," he told my husband.

"How dangerous is the operation?" I asked.

"Well, back surgery has certain risks. But if I operate here in San Salvador, the risks will be reduced. Actually," he said, leaning back in his chair, "there's more danger of your being shot by guerrillas on your way back and forth from Santa Ana than of your husband's dying or being crippled because of this operation."

Small comfort for a scared woman in El Salvador, I thought.

The stars were shining when I left for the hospital on the morning of the operation. Remembering the doctor's words, I committed myself, my husband, and our children to God. At first I felt afraid to be alone out in the darkness, but as I drove toward the capital, I sensed God's presence.

Thinking of God's love, I started singing "Jesus Loves Even Me" then "Oh, How I Love Jesus." I felt so loved that I cried while I sang.

The sun was coming up as I neared the city. Another sunrise was bursting in my heart. I had experienced God's love, presence, and protection. I had long known that God loves me and protects me, but this time I had felt it in my heart.

Jesus said, "I am with you alway" (Matthew 28:20).

Thank You, Lord, for Your loving, comforting presence.

Security

READ: Lamentations 3:22-33

With one hand
He brings
affliction
to me.

With the other hand
He holds me up
in the fiery trial.

That makes me secure
Right in His embrace.

Hold My Hand, Father

READ: Psalm 37:23-28

My three-year-old and I climbed the steep, rocky path to visit a sick lady. Karen stumbled repeatedly, but she didn't fall. I was tightly holding her hand.

It reminded me of a verse I had just read in the Psalms. "Though he fall [trip or stumble], he shall not be utterly cast down [fall headlong]: for the Lord upholdeth him with his hand" (Psalm 37:24).

What sweet comfort to know that God holds my hand! He is able to keep me from falling (Jude 24).

Jesus—In Our Head or Heart?

READ: John 14:15, 21-23

My friend and her husband experienced a renewal in their lives several weeks ago. It was a process that began with confessing their faults to each other and becoming vulnerable and transparent with their friends. God kept them awake most of one night as the healing process continued. Forgiving offenses from childhood, laying their reputation before the Lord, and a desperation for clarity in their relationship with Jesus Christ were all part of the renewal and cleansing. They said, "We feel so CLEAN."

Several days later my friend said to her husband, "I feel like Jesus Christ went from my head to my heart."

I thought about that. I'm still thinking about that. Don't so many "Christians" have Jesus in their heads—and only there? Yes, they know the language, know the right prayers to pray, put on superficial smiles, respond to "How are you?" with "Fine!" even when there's turmoil and hurt inside, can pull out appropriate verses on occasion. Needs? Do they have them? They're not expressed. There's a missing element. What is it? Could it be brokenness? Transparency? Really NEEDING God? Jesus in their heads, yes. Such an experience of Jesus will only reach another head and will result in a head knowledge without a heart experience.

Jesus in the HEARTS of believers . . . that's a LIVING experience! That's where the springs of living water are. That's where the power is—power to forgive, power to lay aside our reputation, power to maintain clarity in our relationship with Him and others, power to risk vulnerability and transparency, power to respond to, "How are you today?" with a "Would you pray for me? I'm struggling," power to confess our faults one to another (that's where the healing begins), power to respond in obedience to the promptings and urgings of the Holy Spirit, power to fall on our faces before Him and say, "God, I NEED YOU." Such an experience of Jesus will reach another heart.

That's what I want—Jesus in my heart.

So help me, God.

He Will Not Remember

READ: Psalm 25:1-7

"Did you hear that Steve was ordained to the ministry?"

"Steve?!"

"Yes, I was surprised too. Why, I remember when we were in Bible school, I thought he was a little wild."

*   *   *   *   *

"*She's* dating your brother? I hope she has grown up since I knew her. I remember when we were young. . . ."

*   *   *   *   *

Such statements prove that often our acts of immaturity are remembered by others long after we wish they would be forgotten. If only I could go back and erase some of the foolish things I said or did. I can imagine people thinking or saying, "*She's* a missionary?! I remember. . . ."

Although it may be impossible to erase those things, I rest in the confidence that God will not remember them against me! They have been removed by the blood of the Crucified One.

54

CHAPTER TWO

She Doeth Him Good
All the Days of Her Life
Proverbs 31:12

Silk and Purple

READ: Proverbs 31:22-25

I wonder why verse 23, "Her husband is known in the gates," is sandwiched between two verses about the virtuous woman's sewing.

Tapestry, silk, and purple. That sounds queenly. Involuntarily I straighten my sagging shoulders. My husband should soon be home from the gates. I must throw out these filthy rags of self-pity that have been cluttering my emotions today. And that grudge looks ugly beside royal apparel. My irritated frown is not becoming to a queen.

Silk and purple are for priestly attire. A servant of the Lord. Holy. Lord make me holy!

My husband is home! His weary eyes light up at my smile. (I threw out the frown just in time.) His manly heart feels battered. The gates are a prime target for public criticism.

I listen. He doesn't need my advice, nor my reminders of his weaknesses. I try to give the loyal words that befit a king. Isn't that my queenly duty?

Days later, he returns to the gates with his spirits lifted. Did I just sell a fine linen girdle? These Indian ladies bunch up their long Mayan skirts and tuck them into their belt to make walking and working easier. Do the silk and purple I wear and the fine linen I make, help my husband fulfill his taxing responsibilities in the gates?

Do I Have to Share Him?

READ: Mark 10:28-31

Now he's mine, I thought on our wedding day. Although I knew that God had first claim on my husband's life, I was unprepared for the implications of that claim.

None of our wedding vows had said anything about sharing my husband. I didn't know then that countless brown-skinned Salvadoreans would soon be taking chunks of my husband's days and nights. I had no idea that he'd become so involved in soul-winning. Nor was I prepared for the long hours he'd spend counseling new Christians.

At first it was hard to accept. I wanted to have first place in my husband's life. I wasn't satisfied with the time he spent with me.

Then I read about Dwight and Mamie Eisenhower. As the story goes, Dwight took Mamie aside soon after their wedding. He told her that his country would have first place and she would have second. Mamie accepted it and they lived together happily for 52 years.

If Mamie Eisenhower could accept second place in her husband's life for the sake of the United States of America, can I do less for the kingdom of God?

Someone once wrote, "It's better to have 10 percent of a 100 percent man than to have 100 percent of a 10 percent man." Thinking of it that way helps me be content even when Eli's not at home.

Yes, my husband is mine. But first of all, he belongs to God. If only I wouldn't forget so often!

Follow the Leader

READ: Ephesians 5:22-33

My husband and I were talking as we walked along the road beside each other. As we drew closer to the village where other eyes would see us, I fell in step behind him. That is the rule of proper etiquette here. I rarely see an Indian woman walking ahead of her husband through the village, to church, or on the plantation trail.

I like that rule. If we are walking through the bush, I have the assurance that no danger is on the path ahead of me. If we are walking through a village, it is much easier for me to follow him to our destination than for him to point it out to me. I like it so well that when we are in the States I find myself following the rule, to my husband's embarrassment. He insists we change rules! We do.

Do I follow the leader in every other area of life? Years ago I came to a satisfying conclusion. When my husband asks me to do something that appears to me unfeasible, somehow if I submit cheerfully, God honors that submission and the result is always best. That includes anything from how to serve food at an Indian wedding to children's bedtime procedures.

Do I always remember that? The Lord has to remind me over and over. He reminds me through

58

His Word and His Spirit. He reminds me when the children say, "Daddy has the most authority," followed by the question, "Mommy, what does authority mean?" But the most painful reminder is when I "walk ahead" and make a wrong turn or encounter a danger for which I am totally unprepared.

The rules of etiquette are not so important. The rules of the Book are all important: "And the wife see that she reverence her husband."

Am I Submissive?

READ: I Timothy 2:9-15

To My Husband,

I realize, Dear, that I have been lax in my submission to you. Not openly rebellious, for I hate the thought of a contentious wife, but subtly in little things. I would never openly defy your authority, but when you asked me to get a letter ready to mail, I pushed it to the back of my mind and planted garden instead. There were some trousers you wanted me to mend, and instead I sewed a new dress for one of the girls. You wanted me to feed the calves. I didn't see any reason one of the children couldn't do it (until a couple of calves died). You asked me to go visiting with you. Inwardly I groaned, wishing I could stay home. Yes, Dear, it's been little things that have eaten away at our relationship.

I commit myself to you anew, not only in noticeable things, but also in the small details which only you and I know about. I promise by the grace of God to do them cheerfully, remembering that my submission to God will be no greater than it is to you.

Gratefully yours,
Your Wife

Peace by Submission

READ: I Corinthians 11:1-10

Have you ever done something for someone without being asked or told just because you knew that's what they wanted you to do—something you really did not want to do? There is peace in this type of submission. It is the kind that God expects of us.

When I married my husband, I thought he had some kind of hang-up about long dresses. His eye seemed to be always on my hemline, and he'd tell me that my dresses were not long enough to suit him. How I would chafe! I didn't like to have to lengthen my dresses even before I wore them! I felt mid-calf was long enough! I told him that I would not mind so much if everyone else at church wore longer than mid-calf dresses. Then submission to his wishes would not be a problem.

Conviction stole over me. Did the Bible say I was to be in submission to my peers? Hardly. Before I could back down on my resolutions, I pulled out several dresses from the wardrobe. Out came the hems. It was work, but I felt a satisfying peace steal over my heart. I was well rewarded for my submission just by this peaceful assurance that I had done the right thing.

Offering Up My Isaac

READ: Genesis 22:1-14

It was past midnight. David was still in his study, getting ready to leave the next morning. He was going to teach at a Bible school over a thousand miles away.

I lay in bed waiting for him to come. Resentment and anger flooded my mind at the thought of his leaving. I was blaming the Bible school directors for asking him to come, the Mission Board for consenting to his going, and my husband for accepting the assignment. The children and I wanted him at home! Our small church needed him too. And aren't there plenty of others who could go?

As the minutes ticked away and sleep was out of sight, the Lord gently broke into my thoughts. "Why are you angry? It's not really the school or the Mission Board who are making him go. It's not even that David wants to be away from his family and the church. I have called him to go. Your husband needs this time with other men of God and youth who are eager to learn. And you need to free him for this. Give David to Me. Offer him up to Me as Abraham did his son Isaac, and I'll give him back to you in a fuller way."

Peace and quietness flooded my being as I let go and said, "Yes, Lord, You're right."

62

David left the next day. The weeks were long, and sometimes I was stretched to the limit in caring for the family, making decisions, and shouldering extra responsibilities. But the Lord's presence was real, and I was given incredible strength and grace to carry on. And when David returned and we were joyfully reunited, it really was true that God gave me back my "Isaac" in a fuller and richer way than before!

In Whatsoever State I Am

READ: Philippians 4:11-13, 19

There are days when I feel like I can't take it any longer. Take yesterday and today for example. Our single fellow is on furlough, so now my husband is the only man on the place, which makes him very busy. In fact, he has people shouting at him from all directions. I'm feeling pushed back and neglected. I haven't had a good chance to talk privately with him for several days. I have needs too and shouldn't I be first in his life? Taking me and the four small children away is such a bother. It's so much easier if we don't go along—but we need outings too! I'm feeling so couped up, and the more I stew about this, the more miserable I feel. Does God care? Does He understand?

*   *   *   *   *

Yes, God understands and cares. He knows my every need. I only need to wait on Him and trust in Him.

This is a day later now. I've had an opportunity to talk with my husband. I was even able to share my feelings of self-pity and rejection without getting all torn up about it. Being understood by one other adult human being helps so much. My heart is blessing God who provides again and again.

My Husband and Others

READ: II Corinthians 4:6-10

My husband is so busy helping others—fixing a tire, arranging for a charter trip, discussing Jesus' teaching in the Sermon on the Mount with a neighbor, preparing for the next service. And he's so busy listening to others—a mother with a report of troubles at school, a neighbor with sickness in his family, a church member with a concern. And he's so busy talking with others— planning a field trip with the teachers, instructing new believers, conversing with those who call, preaching week by week.

When does he have time for me? It seems when we have a moment to talk, someone appears at the door; and when the generator is finally shut down for the night and the doors are locked, we're just too tired to talk. I find myself resenting that others take so much of his time, so much of our time.

But then my husband shares a need he feels or some burden on his heart, and suddenly I take my focus off myself and feel for him and others.

It is then I realize that he does take time for me as well (he washed the dishes while I rested today), that we do have moments to talk uninterrupted (and I need to enjoy them instead of fretting about the time we don't have), that we aren't *always* too tired to talk at the end of the day.

It is then I am grateful that my husband is faithfully fulfilling his calling, and I am willing to help him help others in any way I can.

Hurt by Absences
or Attitudes?

READ: Colossians 3:1-10

I followed my husband into the bedroom. For the fifth evening in a row he was preparing to leave. As the door closed behind us, I said, "Do you have to go again? It seems I always have to put the children to bed by myself. Don't you think your family should come first?"

"Pedro asked me to come this evening. I think he wants to make things right with the Lord again," he said with a sigh. I said no more but left him to finish his preparations.

As he was walking out the door, my daughter said, "Daddy, are you going away again tonight? Why can't you stay at home with us?" I was startled. The complaining note in her voice echoed mine. She sounded so selfish.

As I rocked the baby to sleep to the sound of deep breathing from the other sleeping children, I had time for some serious thoughts. Resentment was welling up in me, resentment that made me blind to the opportunities for good family times. The breakfast table, family worship, or fifteen minutes of pitch-and-catch were just a few of many opportunities for togetherness.

66

Worst of all, my resentment had spilled over into the children's lives. My children were being harmed, not by my husband's frequent evening absences, but by *my* attitudes.

How merciful of my heavenly Father to forgive and cleanse me of my selfishness! With joy I watched loving relationships restored as I submitted to His first claim on my husband and cheerfully supported him.

Anniversary #6

READ: Genesis 2:24; Matthew 19:4-6

Six years ago they promised. They said, "I am" and "I do." They committed themselves to the lordship of Jesus Christ and to each other for a lifetime of loving, sharing, caring, giving, forgiving . . . a new beginning and a happy one.

They joined hands and headed toward the sunrise. Steps were light . . . eyes only for each other . . . laughter, spontaneous. This is living! The path was narrow. That was fine. The closer the better.

Discussion. Quietness. Communication. All were part of the new walking adventure. So MUCH to discover.

An approaching raincloud. Dark sky. Oh. "What do we do now? This is something new." Tears. "Oh, it's so cold and I'm getting wet. I don't like this." "Well, Honey, we'll have to stay together, close for warmth and protection. This too shall pass." Yes, closeness is the word. Togetherness.

Sunshine again. Glorious! They basked. Flowers. Grass greener. All was well.

But while they slept, a windstorm, unexpected. More tears. "Nobody told us we'd have anything like this on our walk. I'm so afraid."

"Honey, it's a way our roots can become strong and

deep. Otherwise our tree will never stand. Let's brave it and stay close. This too shall pass."

There were times when she wandered off on another path. But escape was not the answer. It only produced more fear and less togetherness. He used his special wooing tactics—she ran back to his embrace. Tears. "Forgive me, Honey. I was wrong." Yes, togetherness, not escape, is the answer.

"Oh, we're not alone here, Dear. Others nearby. They're watching. And listening. Where can we hide?" But it was only a narrow road. Nowhere to go. Togetherness again—to withstand pressures of watching eyes and listening ears. To combat the stress of peering people. "This too shall pass."

Yes. There is STRENGTH, hard work, and power in togetherness. They can face anything TOGETHER. They live and learn and grow . . .

. . .committed to togetherness.

CHAPTER THREE

"Her Children Arise Up, and Call Her Blessed"

Proverbs 31:28

71

Only Me

READ: Deuteronomy 6:1-7

While I am washing clothes, the children watch for visitors. One day our son appeared at the door on his tricycle and announced, "There's somebody here, Mom. . . . Only me! Nobody else."

"Only me," yes, only a little boy of mine, but he needs my attention. He needs my time. And yet, so many other things are calling for my attention and time—at mealtimes, family times, in the middle of a job, or at bedtime. It takes wisdom to divide my time with others and still meet the needs of my child.

"Only me"—I must take time for him. I must take time to direct and correct, to see that he obeys the orders I give. I must take time to see that he is learning to be kind and loving, careful and dependable.

I must take time to examine the latest treasure he has found, to listen to his exciting tales of digging a well, to hear what he is saying by his actions as well as his words. I must take time to sing with him, to teach him Bible verses, to tell him Bible stories as he listens, wide-eyed, to bring him to the throne of God in prayer. I must take time to enjoy him, his funny grin, those chubby arms around my neck, his childish joys and excitements. I must take time to answer questions and explain things, to help him understand that Papa is telling someone about Jesus, so he won't be home on time. I must take time to pray for my child.

The Lord knows his needs and cares for him even more than I do, and I need strength and wisdom from above as I seek to guide him day by day.

"Only me," and "only now." I must take time today.

In a Minute

READ: Psalm 104

How many times in the past have I said to one of my children, "In a minute" or, "Let me finish this" or, "Wait a little bit"?

One day I read an article that quoted children's sayings about grandparents. They stated that grandparents have time to take a walk or to look at butterflies with them. Then I thought, *Why do I have to miss this part of my children's lives?*

The next time I started to say, "In a minute," I stopped and went to my children. And what have I discovered since then? A sparrow on our porch, cocking his head this way and that to watch us too. A bed of tulips or irises all abloom. A new leaf just uncurling itself. A wild baby bunny, his heart beating with fear. A bright red cardinal on top of our pine tree. A pile of golden leaves in which to hide. A pumpkin turning orange. The very first snowflakes of the year.

I've found all this and so much more. I've discovered my children—their wonder and delight at each new exploration of this world they live in, their tenderness when they find the small wild animals, the way they quickly grasp the truth that God made all this!

I've also rediscovered God. If God can make a finch

so yellow and black, a cardinal so red and bright, and a sparrow so cheery and chirpy, how much more will He take care of us? Certainly, He will watch over all the small details of our lives.

The next time your children are calling and you say, "In a minute," you may be missing something very important, such as the first bouquet of dandelions in the spring. Yes, dandelions! They are beautiful, too, especially when they are given with hugs and kisses from little arms with the words, "Mom, you're the best mother in all the world because you listen to us. We love you!"

—Deborah Miller. Used by permission.

Challenge by Children

READ: Luke 9:46-48

My son was scanning the sky as the black thunderclouds rolled above us during a spring storm. This was the time of year when tornadoes could come. As the lightning flashed and the thunder rumbled, he remarked, "Well, Mom, all we can do is pray." A lesson in trust. I teach our children to trust in God, but do I trust Him for all of my needs, my daily plans, and the unknown future? Lord, teach me to trust as a little child!

I intervened during a quarrel between my children, mediating a truce. As each asked forgiveness of the other, I marveled how quickly loving feelings were restored. A lesson in forgiveness. Our children forgive in half the time we do. And when they forgive, they at once forget. I struggle with grudges, prejudices, and resentment. Lord, teach me to forgive as a little child.

I was in the midst of disciplining and scolding with a rather loud voice when the phone rang. After I answered in a sweet and kind tone, my daughter remarked about the change in my voice. A lesson in sincerity. I want my children to be free from hypocrisy. Lord, help me to be honest and open as a little child.

Probably the most outstanding lesson Jesus wants

76

us to learn from our children is the lesson of humility. To humble ourselves we must lay aside our anxieties and fears, grudges and prejudices, hypocrisies and insincerities. Stripped of these attitudes, we must let the trustful, forgiving, honest, and loving child live within us.

"I thank thee, O Father, Lord of heaven and earth, because thou hast hid these things from the wise and prudent, and hast revealed them unto babes" (Matthew 11:25).

What Do I Plant?

READ: Proverbs 4:1-13

I sowed some seeds in my garden
In several straight, long rows.
I covered them ever so gently;
By faith I knew they'd grow.

Carefully walking along the edge,
In just a few short days,
I saw the radishes, lettuce, and peas
Peeking through to the sun's warm rays.

Pondering over this miracle,
I wonder how often I've sown
Seeds of discontent and pride
In a child's heart—unknown;

Or if the seeds I've planted there
Were seeds of love and joy,
Which grow with the child and bloom someday,
In a soul, where nought can annoy.

Dear Father, guide my words and acts,
That I may never plant
Weeds in my precious children's hearts.
Wisdom in choices grant.

I want to plant kind, loving deeds
And never hate and strife;
No envious, selfish, thoughtless ways;
But plant eternal life.

It has been said many times, "More is caught than taught." Are there ways I am planting seeds that I won't enjoy reaping someday?

Will my children become discontented because they see I can't do with less than my peers?

Do I give them the smug idea when they do a job well that it was their accomplishment?

Can they catch through my cruel sarcasm that they have a right to feel superior to others?

Am I diligently teaching them where to find peace in these troubled times?

Do they realize that true wisdom from above "is first pure, then peaceable, gentle, and easy to be intreated, full of mercy and good fruits, without partiality, and without hypocrisy" (James 3:17)?

What Are My Priorities?

READ: Job 1:4-5; Matthew 18:1-6

Job has always impressed me. Not only was he devout himself, but he daily offered sacrifices on behalf of his children's spiritual welfare.

The story is told that when a young couple's house caught fire, the wife saved as many of their possessions as she could. Just when she realized the impossibility of reentering the house, she heard her baby crying from his room!

I lost sleep over that one. How could a mother forget her own baby in a crisis such as that? How could she have valued her possessions more than her baby? My children's safety would be my first thought in a situation such as this. In an effort to save my little ones, I would give my life.

Wait a minute. There is no crisis now. Or is there? I am dreadfully busy. I must clean this house today! Why, it's going to seed! What if someone would drop in and see this awful mess? What do I say and do when the children need my attention?

—Susana comes and asks me to please read her a story. It has been a long time since I took time to read to her.

—Marvin is cutting teeth and is so miserable. He just wants to be held.

—Benji comes dragging an afghan. He wants to cuddle awhile.

Now I face the question, which is more important— my children or my house? In the light of eternity, I know. The house can wait. The Lord will understand even if no one else does. My children must take priority over my house.

Spiritual Nutrition

READ: Mark 2:1-12; Luke 4:18

A few years ago, one of the children had a spot on her tongue that kept peeling. As soon as it was healed, the process started all over again. Since it seemed to be quite irritating to her, I took her to our pediatrician to have it checked out. He diagnosed it as a nutritional deficiency. This, of course, was a little embarrassing to me. I felt like it was a reflection on me for not seeing that she had proper nutrition. She never was an overly aggressive eater. He prescribed a vitamin supplement for her, and after several months the problem cleared up.

Most of us are quite concerned about our children's physical health. In the cold winter months, when the sun doesn't shine very long, we are apt to give a vitamin supplement or cook extra-nutritious meals to ward off the many bugs which seem to be so prevalent during that time.

How concerned am I about my children's spiritual nutrition? It is our duty as parents to teach our children there is power in prayer. It is our duty to provide good reading material. It is our duty to encourage them to study the heroes of faith in Hebrews 11. It is our duty to see that they learn about those who gave their lives for the faith. All this is not only our duty, but it is a privilege. In addition to teaching line upon line, we need to be an example of those things which we are teaching. During those times when the clouds of discouragement threaten to take away our peace, our children need to see us saturating our souls with God's Word. When God seems far away and we may not feel like praying, they need to see us providing for extra nutrition for that part of us which is unseen.

Keep the Faith

READ: II Timothy 1:1-6

The importance of a grandmother's role in teaching the Gospel to two or three generations can be seen in the life of Timothy. His grandmother Lois, a widow, taught her daughter, Eunice, who then passed on the sincere faith to grandson Timothy. As a boy, Timothy knew the Scriptures even though his Greek father was an unbeliever. Apparently, both Lois and Eunice had grounded Timothy from childhood in his Biblical heritage.

There is a Scriptural warning of what happens when one generation breaks faith with God and does not keep His commandments or teach them to the following generations:

"So these nations feared the Lord, and served their graven images, both their children, and their children's children: as did their fathers, so do they unto this day" (II Kings 17:41).

However, those who pass on the faith to future generations have the assurance of God's blessing on their children's children:

"But the mercy of the Lord is from everlasting to everlasting upon them that fear him, and his righteousness unto children's children" (Psalm 103:17).

We can be like Lois, faithful in passing on her faith and her knowledge of the Scriptures. Keep the faith!

Bringing Our Children to Jesus

(A Meditation for a Baby Shower)

READ: Mark 10:13-16

What mother isn't touched by the story of Jesus blessing the little children! How we would love to have been one of those mothers. Just to see His look of love and to have His hands lovingly reach out and touch our little ones would have made an unforgettable memory.

But even back then there were hindrances for the mothers. Can you imagine anyone trying to keep children from coming to Jesus? The disciples did. But Jesus intervened, and the mothers were able to bring their little ones to Him so He could hold them in His arms and bless them.

What about us? Are there situations and people who are trying to keep us from bringing our children to Jesus, too? Our work, our preoccupation with our own thoughts, other people, and even our own lack of close fellowship with Jesus can prevent our children from seeing Jesus and being touched by Him.

But if we really want to, we can find many ways to bring our children to Jesus. We can sing with them, tell them Bible stories, and talk freely about Jesus in everyday experiences. As we go on nature walks or look at the moon and stars on a clear night, we can tell them who made all these things. We can pray with them at bedtime, mealtime, and family sharing times. In times of trouble as well as in happy times, we can spontaneously turn to Jesus as the One who cares and understands. And in our personal time with the Lord, we can lift our children up individually, every day, and ask the Lord to touch and bless them.

Someone has said, "Once a mother, always a mother." So our task and privilege of coming to Jesus with our children never ends. All our life we can keep bringing them to Him by our prayers, and guiding them to Him by our own example of going to Him for blessing and guidance. What a privilege we have!

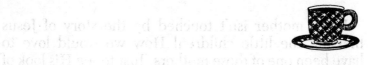

"The Lord Lift Up His Countenance Upon Thee"

READ: Numbers 6:23-27

As a mother of three preschoolers, I was often discouraged by all I *could* be doing. There were young Christians to visit and encourage, sick ones in the village who could perhaps be won to the kingdom if I would be able to minister to their bodily needs. Oh, I could see so many opportunities for service. But with three little ones to care for, there was little time left to do things for others.

Some of my discouragement crept into a letter I sent to a friend. Her answer was not slow in coming.

"Our position in relation to the sun determines where our shadow falls. The same is true in a spiritual sense.

"The daily duties of raising children sometimes seem to be a heavy burden, keeping us from serving the Lord in 'more important' ways. But if we keep standing in the right position to the Son, our shadow of influence will have the right effect on our children. They will go places and do things for the Lord we never can.

"Which is more valuable? The doing or the influence? The first will not happen without the second." *
* Romaine Stauffer

87

Ashamed of God's Gifts?

READ: Psalm 127

I was ashamed of myself! Whatever possessed me to say what I did? Seeing me with two active pre-schoolers and a baby in my arms, a friend remarked, "Looks as if the Lord has blessed you with three little angels." My response was in a negative tone. She laughed. But as I reflected, I felt guilty, for I realized this was not an isolated case. Even though I loved babies and our children were very dear to me, I felt a bit embarrassed that they were so close in age.

Would I be ashamed of a gift given to me by a close friend? Of course not. I like to display such a gift because I want others to know that someone cared enough to give it to me. Then why am I embarrassed about the blessings God has given us? Why must I feel that I should apologize to others whenever they comment about our children? Is it because it isn't the world's practice to have very many children? Are the ideas of the world creeping into my heart?

When I heard a brother telling about how the Lord had blessed them with two lovely daughters, my heart swelled. That was the attitude to possess. We need never be ashamed that God has blessed us with our priceless gifts. After all, children are a heritage from Him!

Bedtime ☆

READ: Genesis 33:1-7

It's bedtime.
I'm fatigued by this heat.
But there is a bedtime story to read, prayers to pray, teeth to brush, drinks to get, children to escort to bed, and Baby to rock. Then there is the question-and-comment session after everyone is in bed and *supposed* to be asleep.

Frequently I wish there were a switch to pull or button to push that would land the children in bed immediately and safely asleep. Oh for quiet time to read a book, write, or just go to bed.

Then I think of my little boy who will never need to be put to bed again. What would I give to hear his long prayers for all his friends? Or to kiss him good night? Or feel his squeeze? Just once more.

I think of other mothers who would love to put their children to bed with full tummies, or the promise of Daddy's soon return. I think of others who have never had a child to tuck into bed.

I give thanks and cherish bedtimes.

Yes, even when I hear "Mommy?" for the tenth time after all the heads are nestled on their pillows.

Yelling at Youngsters

READ: Isaiah 11:1-6

Visions of being the ideal mother were mine. A super mom. So I was never going to yell at my children. Yesterday I did it again.

Then my five-year-old said, "Mama, I feel you don't love me when you talk to me like that."

Oh, ouch. I *felt* that. A super mom? My daughter doesn't think so evidently. I sat down, brought her close, and said, "Sweetheart, I was wrong. Jesus doesn't want me to talk to you like that. I listened to the devil and that's not good. Forgive me. Let's ask Jesus to forgive me, too."

She understood, forgave, and promised to pray for me. I was so touched . . . and humbled.

A super mom? No, my children will not see me like that. But I want them to see a mother who fears the Lord, who seeks Him with all her heart, and who is never too proud to say, "I'm sorry. I was wrong. Forgive me."

God can extend His grace again and again to such a mother. And grace is what I need. Grace—the power of God in my life, doing what I can't do. Grace to love again and again. Grace to be patient and gentle. Grace to listen to questions and answer them. Grace not to yell but to have the law of kindness on my tongue.

90

Grace to read stories and more stories. Grace to put the Word into them at every opportunity.

Then I think of my Father. He never yells at me. When I come to Him and say, "God, I've done it again," He says, "What have you done? I forgave you the last time and I don't remember."

He doesn't even yell at me, "I told you so. Why didn't you try Me *first?* Won't you ever learn?"

I've come to see that my Father delights in seeing me come to the end of myself. "God, I'm finished. I can't do it. I need YOU."

A super mom? No. I need help. I need Jesus. I want my children to see that—so they'll know where to go, too.

A super Father? Yes. MY Father.

Building Memories

READ: Deuteronomy 4:5-10

As we look back into our childhood, we remember those happy, special family times. It is important to build memories for our children, and the mission field lends many opportunities to do so! Let me share a few memories our grown children reminisce and laugh about.

Our camping trips are a number-one family memory—the fun of spending a few days in a tent, out along the sea or at Mountain Pine Ridge, with Dad doing the cooking, enjoying the specialties of potato chips, candy, etc. Happy times, laughing and playing together!

Christmastime brings many fond memories. Caroling and sharing fruit baskets, visiting and having people drop in for light cake and fantas, the delight of eating apples, a pear, and grapes (a once-a-year luxury) are special, never-forgotten family traditions. The first year we lived back in the States, I was so happy that our children could experience a real Christmas with grandparents and cousins, but that evening our son remarked, "This didn't seem like Christmas!" Now we are dreaming of someday returning to Belize with our whole family for Christmas!

Gardening was a family project. How pleased our

children were with the few vegetables we harvested. Just recently one of them recalled the exact number of quarts of string beans I canned one year!

Trips to town, a banana from their special friend in the market, dinner in a restaurant, picking up the mail—our one son remembers with fondness the occasional loaf of bread we purchased in town, compared to the hundreds of loaves I baked!

Happy memories will bond our children to us and keep their hearts tender as we share Christ's love with them!

Deprived or Privileged?

READ: Luke 1:67-80

John the Baptist "grew, and waxed strong in spirit
. . . **in the deserts** . . ." (Luke 1:80). I wonder if
Zacharias and Elisabeth ever worried about their son
being deprived or becoming a "loner." Maybe not,
because they knew even before his birth what his
mission in life was to be.

But what about us? No doubt all missionary parents
are concerned about the effect their calling and lifestyle will have on their children. Will they be
deprived or even ruined by living in the "desert,"
away from the nourishing effects of grandparents,
good schools, youth groups, and cultural opportunities?

It may mean not seeing a single relative for a year or
more. A teenager may spend many lonely Sunday
afternoons in his room reading or writing because
there is no place to go and no close friend to be with.
The children will see much sin around them and hear
of violence and tragic deaths of people they know well.

But being a missionary child is not all negative, and
there are many blessings and added bonuses. Having
lived in a cross-cultural setting has helped some of our
children, who are now in service themselves, to relate
to yet another culture. Missionary children often

observe firsthand the change in people's lives as they become Christians. They also develop a real burden for unsaved friends. Being more isolated has also encouraged us in much close family living and in being creative in providing our own entertainment. It's very important for parents not to develop a "you poor children" attitude. We need to focus on the benefits and blessings, involve them in our ministry, and pray for them daily!

We know that the Lord who has called us is well able to keep our children in any situation, whether we are missionaries or not. So, whether our children grow up in the deserts of isolation or in rich social pastures, they all need to drink the fresh springs of living water in order to grow and become strong in spirit like John the Baptist.

Missionary Children

READ: Daniel 1:3-17

"Don't you think you should return to the States for the sake of your children?" some people ask.

Should we?

God called my husband and me to El Salvador. He gave us children. Can we not trust Him to meet our children's needs here?

We are thankful for the privilege of rearing children on the mission field.

Missionary children have opportunities to expand life's horizons beyond that of the average child. They have many cross-cultural experiences. They learn second or third languages. Lots of travel gives them a broader view of the world.

I consider homeschooling another big advantage. I like to teach my own. A special relationship develops as we study together.

The most important advantage to missionary children may be in the area of spiritual development. Their faith has been tested. They've seen miraculous answers to prayer and God's power to change lives. They usually become involved in soul-winning and follow-up at an earlier age. Early responsibility in the church fosters maturity.

Aren't there many dangers, though? Yes, there are.

A former missionary said, "I can't tell you there aren't dangers on the mission field. But there are also dangers in the States."

No matter where we rear our children, we need God's abundant grace and wisdom. He promised in James 1:5, "If any of you lack wisdom, let him ask of God, that giveth to all men liberally, and upbraideth not; and it shall be given him."

"Lord, thank You for our children. Give us wisdom to bring them up for You, no matter where we live."

Popsicles or Eternal Riches?

READ: Philippians 3:7-14

We had just returned to Belize after a furlough, when one of our boys asked, "What was the thing we ate in the States—it was on a stick and tasted like ice cream?" After I reminded him that it was called a popsicle, I pondered in my heart: were we depriving our children of the simple things that had been a part of my own childhood, like popsicles or good times spent with grandparents and cousins, or better education, etc.?

But I am convinced that God has brought special blessings into the lives of our children, intangible riches, experiences that I never experienced as a child, such as:

—a new world, things I only studied about in geography

—travel experience by plane, bus, dugout, ferries, passenger trucks, and many others

—friends with different skin color; they don't even notice the difference

—joy in simple things such as climbing trees, catching iguanas, playing marbles, making slingshots, etc.

—a concern for the lost—at a very young age, a familiar question rises, "Is he a Christian?"

Whosoever will save his children may lose them, but whosoever is willing to lose his children for Christ's sake will keep them!

End of the Rope

READ: I Samuel 1

For days the calf begged to be released from his pen. He wanted to savor the luscious green grass. One day my husband tied a rope to his neck and fastened the other end to the mango tree. I expected the calf to revel in his new freedom and opportunities immediately. But I was surprised. He ran to the end of his rope and stood there bawling. The lush, nutritious grass was not enough. He wanted the wide world.

I was released from the pen of childhood and put into the rich pasture of motherhood. But how many times have I stood at the end of the rope and bawled for greater opportunities out there? How often have I felt tied down to answering endless childish questions? Standing still when I wished to be running to serve in "more important" ways?

When I get to the end of the rope and start bawling, I remember what a brother once told me. "We get in a hurry. When God needed a prophet and a judge, He chose a Hannah. When He needed a Saviour, He chose a Mary. He chose a woman, not to be the judge, prophet, or Saviour, but to bear and mother a son."

So little mother, tie the apron strings tighter. Back to washing faces and answering little ones' questions about God. Back to sewing dresses and teaching the

99

reasons for nonconformity to the world. Back to tucking shirts in pants and teaching why we don't use the swear words other little boys use.

"In due season you will reap." Can you wait the season?

Who Controls My Life?

READ: Psalm 113

I thought I had control of my life. Our first two children were prayed for, planned for, and born on schedule. When the third pregnancy ended soon after it began, I felt that I just wasn't ready for another pregnancy for a long time. After all, I reasoned, my body and mind needed to recuperate from such a traumatic experience.

Three months is not a long time, but God overruled my plans. I was expecting again! Of course, negative thoughts crowded my mind. I felt guilty because I couldn't feel the maternal love flowing to my unborn child as I had felt with my other children. Suppose I wouldn't be able to love this baby enough?

After much heart struggle, I was able to cast these cares upon the Lord and look forward to the birth of my child.

Time has flown and our son has grown rapidly. Why the Lord saw fit to send him along when He did, I may never know. Perhaps it was to help me realize that He is the One in control, not I. This child has brought so much joy into our lives that I often wonder why I ever felt the way I did. I am grateful that God's thoughts and ways are extremely superior to mine.

At the Birth of a Firstborn

READ: Luke 1:28, 39-56

It was 2:30 a.m. I had just finished feeding our tiny firstborn son who was only two days old. I was far away from my mother. How I would have loved to have her with me in this first-time experience of motherhood! (Do we ever appreciate our mothers more than when we first become mothers?!) As I pondered the miracle and marvel of birth and being a mother, my hospital room became an almost sacred place. Everything was so quiet, and I wanted to hold the memory of this moment forever. So I reached for a pen and paper and wrote:

> Ah! now it's mine!
> To wear the sacred crown of Motherhood.
> For nine long months we worked together,
> My God and I,
> To form this brand-new life so different.
>
> Oh! sacred trust!
> To wear this noble crown reserved for us
> Who now can know a little of the love
> Which God did feel
> When He created man at first.

This little babe!
How trustful and content he seems
When in my arms he snuggles close.
No fear has he
What could befall in years ahead.

Oh! teach me on!
My little one who's come to me from God.
Show me how to put such trust in God above
Who loves me so,
And never fear what future days will hold.

Legacy of an Adopted Child

READ: Esther 2:5-11

Once there were two women who never knew each
other;
One you do not remember; the other you call mother.
One gave you a nationality; the other gave you a name;
One gave you the seed of talent; the other gave you an
aim.

Two different lives shaped to make yours one.
One became your guiding star, the other became your
sun.
One gave you emotions; the other calmed your fears.
One saw your first sweet smile; the other dried your tears.

The first gave you life and the second taught you how
to live in it.
The first gave you a need for love and the second was
there to give it.
One gave you up; it was all she could do.
The other prayed for a child, and God led her straight
to you.

And now you ask me through your tears
The age-old question through the years;
Heredity or Environment, which are you a product of?

Neither, my darling, neither.
Just two different kinds of Love!

—Anonymous

"Thank You, Lord, for your special way of bringing children and parents together who need each other."

CHAPTER FOUR

"We Are Labourers Together With God"

I Corinthians 3:9

Workers Together

READ: Ephesians 4:13-16

Fellow workers. What can I say? They are going to read this. If I only praise, I am insincere. If I only criticize, I expose myself. The faults I most despise in others are the ones I am most guilty of myself. Why does it work that way?

Here I often meet up again with Dad's idiosyncrasies, my brother's disgusting habit, my sister's untouchable spot, or Mom's touchy spot—among fellow missionaries. I should have done my homework in interpersonal relationships years ago. That's why God designed my family.

I see new workers full of enthusiastic idealism. I'm embarrassed to recall my own falls and bumps as a missionary "toddler." I see older workers unimpressed by modern mission lingo: world view, contextualization, bonding. Their quiet fruits prove that prayer, faith, and love will never grow obsolete in successful mission work. I see a martyred look and am desperate to know where I offended so I can clear the air. Another sister tells me point-blank. That ouches, too.

Fellow workers. These are my equals. I cannot talk down to them like illiterates, nor up to them like government officials. We level. That is delicate communication. It is bombarded by Satan. By prayer, we enjoy a rare friendship. We are committed to each other. Fragile feelings? Yes, because the opinions of these great people are exceedingly valuable to me.

A Special Person

READ: I Corinthians 3:3-9

She is my helper—
  ready to help with unexpected guests
  or to peel mangoes and can pineapples,
  cheerfully lending me some sugar or
  baking a batch of cookies!

She is a substitute aunt to our children—
  playing with them, listening to their
  problems, encouraging them;
  sometimes she may even need to
  discipline, but they still love her!

She is my friend—
  when I need a listening ear,
  or I'm homesick and frustrated
  and blue,
  we share our joys and sorrows!

She is my co-worker—
  her world is my world;
  we work together,
  pray together, and cry together!

She is the single girl working with us—
  and I will be *her* helper, helping when
   her work is more than *she* can handle;

109

I will be a sister to *her,* encouraging and
    loving *her;*

I will be *her* friend when she's had bad news
    from home or is homesick and blue;
I will remember we are co-workers, laboring
    together for the cause of Christ!

Co-workers

READ: Galatians 5:22-26

With interest I read the article on Baron Bliss, benefactor of Belize. "He even figured out a way to pipe fresh water aboard his yacht without going ashore," I related to my husband.

"I read that too. The man was too lazy to get off his boat," Jason said a bit scornfully.

"But he was crippled and on a wheelchair," I pointed out.

"Oh, is that right? I didn't read that part," he replied. Now that he had the whole picture, he saw Baron Bliss, not as a lazy nobleman, but as a courageous, ingenious individual.

How many times have I seen my fellow workers in the same way? "Why did she tell that lady the opposite of what I said?" "Why did he do what we agreed among ourselves not to do?" "Why do they get a vacation *now*?"

When that happens, I want to remember three things.

First, I am seeing only part of the picture. If I understood everything in the situation, I would probably see their actions differently.

Second, they have probably been in the same situation and wondered why I did what I did. So it's a

111

reminder to me to be careful.

And third, even if I don't understand, I still need these verses:

—"We are labourers together with God" (I Corinthians 3:9).

—"So we, being many, are one body in Christ, and every one members one of another" (Romans 12:5).

—"Charity [love] . . . beareth all things [is always patient], believeth all things [is always loyal], hopeth all things [always expects the best], endureth all things [is always supportive]" (I Corinthians 13:4, 7).

In Times of Sickness

READ: Matthew 25:34-40

I am not surprised that Jesus included "I was sick, and ye visited me" (Matthew 25:36) as worthy of mention when He recognizes His children at the judgment. It means so much to all of us to have someone care and help out in times of sickness.

This is especially true for missionaries who are far from "home" and their natural family. Having co-workers step in and become "family" is a precious thing indeed. I want to tell you about two different times when this happened to us.

Our third child was born the first summer we were in the North. When he was ten days old, I suddenly had to return to our small Red Cross hospital for observation and then surgery. I wasn't allowed to have my baby with me, so a dear sister offered to care for him. Others helped with the housework and looked after our two- and four-year-olds when David came in to visit me.

The second incident was when I was in the hospital for several weeks after a car accident. I had many persons from the community and fellow missionaries and even my sister from the States to visit me. But I think especially of three single workers who came to visit regularly. Each had her unique ministry to me.

113

One was a nurse and could answer all those special questions I had. She reassured me many times. The second one often ministered to me in a spiritual way with just the right words of hope and comfort. And the third one had such a pleasant and cheerful disposition. She brought bits of news and conversation that always brightened my day.

"Lord, thank You for those who have ministered to us in times of sickness, and help us to be sensitive to do the same."

Little Notes

READ: Philemon 3-7

I found a cheery note on my desk the other day. A co-worker put it there for me. How it brightened my day! On other occasions I've found notes on the bookshelf, in the cupboard, and on the dresser.

We all need encouragement, reassurance, and love. Notes of appreciation, words of cheer, and expressions of sympathetic understanding mean so much. Little notes can be big aids to interpersonal relationships.

The Bible says, "But to do good and to communicate forget not: for with such sacrifices God is well pleased" (Hebrews 13:16).

Excuse me, please. I need to write a little note right now.

Rest Your Mind

READ: I John 3:11-19

One morning after my husband left, I noticed that one of the workers wasn't doing what I remembered my husband had assigned. I found myself stewing and brewing, and finally decided to go ask him kindly if he knew that my husband wanted the other job done.

On my way out, I slowed my steps and stopped. This was not my business. Back to the house I went.

So now since it was not my business to say something to the worker, it was not for me to stew about it either. So I prayed about it, placing it in the Lord's hands, and rested my mind. (Later I found out that this worker was doing what he was supposed to do that day.)

It's easy to burden our minds with a list of irritations and annoyances when we work so closely with others and get to know each other so well. How good to rest our minds instead by being kind in our thoughts toward others, overlooking faults, letting annoyances pass, and being fair in our judgment. These things shall pass, and what shall we remember of the past? Our irritation and unforgiving spirit? Or, will we use these opportunities to practice the golden rule and go the second mile in our relationships? As members of God's family, we are committed to each other and committed to the way of love Christ taught and lived before us. As we strive to follow Christ in this way, we will find more peaceful relationships with others. Our own hearts will be at peace and our minds at rest.

The Bumper Sticker's Lesson

READ: Philippians 2:5-11

The airport intercom interrupted my thoughts, tightening the knot in my stomach. She had just arrived, the former worker with whom I had had some conflicts. How would I react to her? Was she still angry with me? What would become of our relationship?

With clammy hands, I fumbled for my keys. It was time to take the car to the passenger exit. I worried all the way to the parking lot. Then I saw it. On the car next to ours was a bumper sticker. "JESUS IS LORD," it said. As I read and reread those words, the tension drained from the back of my neck. A strange peace filled me.

"Of course," I reminded myself, "Jesus is Lord. He's Lord of my life, Lord of my reactions, Lord of my relationships. He is Lord of all. With His help, everything will turn out all right."

And it did.

The Molehill Problem

READ: I Thessalonians 4:1, 2, 9-11

I should have discussed the matter with my speedy co-worker, but I kept putting it off. There she was slaving away from morning till night. She was getting a host of things done while the little I got done in a day's time was to take care of my family and a FEW other odds and ends. It seemed this area of work was a hobby of hers, and I didn't know if she thought I should help. I just didn't know what she was thinking. Eventually I started imagining this and that and the other thing about what she must think of slow me.

Finally, after many moons of this, I decided to talk to my single co-worker instead of letting the situation drag on any longer. I was so surprised to discover that she merely enjoyed the challenge and didn't hold any feelings against me for my lack of assistance. Oh, the joy of knowing everything was all right! I could have enjoyed God's peace from the start in this area if I had just been willing to talk to my fellow worker.

But why had I let it go so long?

Burden Bearing

READ: Matthew 11:25-30

Burden bearing. Encouraging. Interceding. Lifting up. Listening. Sometimes we are on the receiving end, and other times we are the one who is giving. All of us can be a part of this sharing. I'm sure Jesus never intended that we carry all our burdens by ourselves.

A fellow missionary phones at 12:30 a.m. to ask us to pray for them *right now.* Her husband needs wisdom and protection in dealing with a suicidal and (apparently) demonically oppressed person.

As Lowell leaves for school, he turns and says, "Mom, pray for me today. I have a hard algebra test."

I am anxious as my husband is flying to isolated villages and the weather doesn't look too favorable for flying. A native sister assures me that she always prays for David as he goes out.

After two hours of listening to and sharing with a lady about her difficult marriage and personal conflicts, I hear her say, "I feel so much better about it now," even though her situation hasn't changed at all outwardly.

Our Bible study group prayed for Evelyn when she was undergoing tests for a lung ailment. Together we faced the possibility of lung cancer and perhaps even death for her. Later, when we found out the results of

119

the tests, we rejoiced that it was a parasitic cyst instead.

Our daughter is burdened about a relationship at work and asks that I pray for her.

There are some burdens we feel we can't share with anyone. But praise the Lord, we have an always available Burden Bearer, the One with whom we are yoked together. And if we are so burdened that we can't even carry our part of the yoke, we can accept the invitation to cast all our cares on Him, because He cares for us (I Peter 5:7).

In a Hurry

READ: Isaiah 26:5-9

"Always in a hurry—and plenty of time for others, but none for me." One of my missionary friends was just like that. We never had time together in a relaxed way, and I found it annoying. And, yes, it even hurt!

This relationship was so upsetting I finally began wondering if *I* treated any of my friends in this same hurried, preoccupied way. An evaluation of my friendships seemed to confirm my suspicions! Many of my relationships were shallow, uncaring, and selfish.

As I made an effort to be more sensitive and warm in my contacts with others, the Lord showed me how my relationship with Him was always in a hurry too! Ouch! But it was true. Often I would quickly slide through my devotions without much thought and rush off.

In retrospect it became clear that my faulty devotional life had created a spiritual vacuum in my life. The self-centered preoccupation with my needs (that goes with a spiritual vacuum) had left me both insensitive and vulnerable. I was insensitive to the needs of those around me, and paradoxically, quite vulnerable to the way others responded to me.

Of Steps and Souls

READ: Ephesians 4:1-7

The two children eagerly agreed to my suggestion to scrub the steps. I equipped them with scrub brushes, soapy water, a cup, and clean water for rinsing. Enthusiasm was high as I showed them how to do the first step, and they took over with a will. All went well as they concentrated on making the steps nice and clean for Mommy, and I listened with joy as they eagerly encouraged each other. But by the time they reached the fifth step, I heard some discordant sounds. They were arguing about which brush was working better, who should have the best one, and who was doing it the right way.

My presence at the head of the stairs and a few kindly words of instruction, along with the reminder of the goal (clean steps) set things in order once more. It stayed that way for only two steps. Then I heard the same quarrelsome notes again. Now one was rinsing where the other hadn't washed. Oh, there were so many things to argue about: who was getting dirtier, who was working hardest, who wasn't doing the job thoroughly.

Children, yes, children. Are we "like unto children sitting in the marketplace, and calling one to another, and saying, We have piped unto you, and ye have not

122

danced" (Luke 7:32)? How often have I heard debates on methods and means of mission work! The clashing sounds have arisen over many issues. Shall we give material aid or only spiritual help? Shall we concentrate on children or adults? What shall our standard of living be? The list is endless. How rasping the sounds must be on the ears of our Father!

He has entrusted us with a work—the bringing of souls to Him. To achieve the goal He has fully equipped us, even to the extent of bestowing differing gifts. If we neglect the goal in our concern over the *methods* of reaching the goal, our disharmony is our defeat.

A Missionary's Plea

READ: II Corinthians 1:8-11

I had a need so desperate
  That God alone did know—
In great love and boundless mercy
  He saw me in my woe.
He knew that all my strength was spent
  And I was sore distressed;
But too, He knew I'd worked and prayed
  And done my very best.
Thus as I struggled with my fears,
  I thought about my brothers
And prayed to God in faith and hope
  To lay my cares on others.
And so He prompted them to pray;
  The Spirit gave them utterance.
Then as their prayers went heavenward,
  My heavy load seemed light;
My strength and zeal returned again;
  The enemy took flight.
My soul is blessed; my mind is clear;
  The tasks seem not so great;
For there are those who pray for me
  And on the Spirit wait.
They get few letters from my pen,
  For to God I send my plea.
He hears and moves upon their hearts,
  And they share this work with me.

—Revised by V. Swartzentruber

124

CHAPTER FIVE

*"He . . . Hath Broken Down
the Middle Wall of Partition"*

Ephesians 2:14

Our Lowly Nature He Hath Not Abhorred

READ: Ephesians 2:1-6

She lay on our couch in the living room, coughing up gray corruption. I gave her a can so she wouldn't spit on the floor. She smelled like she needed a bath. Her shriveled face had no comeliness that we should desire her. Did she have tuberculosis? Or was her alcoholic life aging her prematurely?

I needed to hear something besides that gagging. Christmas carols! I turned on the tape player that my husband had adapted to the two-way radio battery.

Cheerful anthems filled this house. "O come all ye faithful . . . our lowly nature He hath not abhorred." It startled me.

In a flash I saw a holy God, high and lifted up. I saw myself, filthy and abhorred. I saw Jesus in an eternity of mercy, spanning the unspannable between a perfect God and a worthless me. I looked at the racking creature on the couch. Suddenly our differences didn't seem so great after all.

Fifty Cents for a Friendship

READ: Proverbs 27:1-17

It was a typical Monday morning. You know: a bit hectic, quite busy, dishes still waiting, baby needing attention, Mom not exactly in the mood for a visit.

But my Christian sister came anyway, so I asked her in and invited her to sit down. "I won't stay long," she said. "I want to settle my credit with you."

Well, that was a nice Monday morning treat. I was glad to do that. So I got the credit book and went over the figures. I noticed one item was a cake I had baked for them. Mentally I recalled it—a flat, chocolate one that hadn't turned out very nice. "I'll only charge you two dollars for the cake instead of two-fifty," I told her. "It wasn't very nice."

"Okay, good," she replied.

After we had settled her account, she wondered if I still had the cloth remnants I had showed her several days before. I did, so I brought them out for her to go through again. Selecting one piece, she asked me the price. Since it wasn't quite a yard I told her it would be two-fifty rather than the usual three dollars.

"But you said the other day that piece would be two dollars," she said.

Anger, disgust, and perhaps a few other emotions surged up instantly inside of me. I tried not to show

127

too much of my feelings as I replied, "Very well, then it's two dollars."

After she left, I continued to rehash the happening. Just to think that I had been generous enough to knock off fifty cents from the cake, and she had had the nerve to tell me I had asked fifty cents too much for a piece of cloth. I had forgotten the price I had quoted her earlier but she hadn't. Round and round and on and on my thoughts went.

But then the Holy Spirit stopped me in my mental tracks. "Is fifty cents a fair price to pay for this friendship?" He asked. "If you hold this incident against her, you won't enjoy being her friend anymore. You won't feel good toward her. You won't want to help her or be glad to see her come."

I thought about His words. I thought about my soul and her soul. I thought about eternity. I decided fifty cents was a small price to pay for forgiveness and peace.

When Cultures Meet

READ: Ruth 2

What happens when two rivers meet? What happens when two people meet in the bond of marriage? What happens when two different cultures meet? Often there is turbulence.

I am tempted to think, "If he would just consider my upbringing and do things *my* way . . ." or, "If they would just cooperate and understand me. . . ."

For the river of marriage to flow smoothly, there must be a yielding. Yielding on *my* part. The same is true in cultures. For blending to take place, I must yield to another culture.

If I consider the things about myself that are irritating to others, the blending will be easier. How do they view my care of possessions, my use of time? What about my attitude toward their country and fellow countrywomen?

Last week the maid and I sang together,
"Let me be a little kinder,
 Let me be a little blinder,
 To the faults of those about me. . . ."

That is my answer. Kindness is the perfect blender of cultures.

"Let me be humble enough to be enriched by what someone else is that I am not." *

* © 1976 by Elizabeth Elliot in *Twelve Baskets of Crumbs,* published by Christian Herald House, Chappaqua, NY 10514.

Those Hired Girls!

READ: Luke 6:31, 40-42

Most of us who have spent time on the mission field know the ups and downs of having hired girls to help with our domestic duties. While we were grateful for their help and felt we could hardly do without them, there were also times of frustration, times when they just did not live up to our expectations. I would get so irked at my hired girls when I gave them explicit instructions and it seemed they deliberately went against my wishes.

*   *   *   *   *   *   *

Then the scene changed. Between terms in Guatemala we were in Maryland on a dairy farm. No hired girls. Now I needed to go out in the afternoons to help milk. Oh, there was so much to learn!

As the list of instructions went on, my head began to swim. How could I ever remember all this? Trying to remember the order in which I was to wash the cows, I heard my husband's voice breaking through the jumble of my thoughts.

Then I realized I had left a milker on too long. Instead of removing it immediately as I had been told, I had washed another cow first. In addition to that, I had forgotten to check for mastitis.

Whoops! I keep on making mistakes. I know I am being more bother than I am worth.

To my surprise, my dear husband actually thanked me for all my help! He discredited my assertion that I didn't help very much.

Then I thought of my hired girls. With shame I knew that I had not been as patient with them as I should have been. Perhaps they felt the same way I did with all those detailed instructions.

"Thank You, God, for putting me in the place of the 'helper.' Thanks for teaching me the golden rule. I shall remember that lesson a long time."

The Way to a Man's Heart Is Through His Stomach

READ: I Corinthians 9:19-27

Kekchi Fellowship meetings. Fellowship! I sure don't feel a speck of it at this moment between my brown sisters and me. When will they ever learn to serve food efficiently so they can get back to the meeting? Don't they realize the importance of hearing God's Word?

Chagrined, I admit the preaching isn't doing me much good right now even if I am sitting in service. My thoughts are far too chaotic to concentrate on the Kekchi message.

Next day, here come all the sisters who cooked and served to wash the dishes. As the last sticky grain of rice is scrubbed away, I approach a necessary subject.

"Sisters, please forgive me for my impatient words these last three days."

Forgiveness is graciously granted. Then they drift off into Kekchi, in an animated discussion. I listen closely.

"See how God is working. Some folks came to service for the first time. But it is also the first time they saw food lines. Some were angry and offended because they didn't understand. It is important we

132

serve their food kindly so they will receive the Word of God."

And here I had been concerned about serving efficiently so they'd have time to hear the Word.

Sure, some come only for the loaves and fishes. But HOW we give the loaves and fishes might be the only Gospel message they will ever hear.

The Generosity of the Poor

READ: John 12:1-8

A native girl gave Karen a beautiful new doll.
Rosalva had gotten it for Christmas. Her act of love
overwhelms me.

Why do the poor give us so much? How can we
respond to their gifts? We, who have so much, hate to
accept gifts from them, especially such valuable gifts.

Still, it would be unthinkable to refuse their presents. How deeply it would hurt them! The only proper
thing to do is to accept the gifts with gratitude. We can
show, with words and actions, how much we appreciate their generosity.

Why am I so selfish? The natives put me to shame. I
want to learn from them to give my best to others.
A beautiful doll named Rosalva will help me to
remember.

Rich Americans

READ: II Corinthians 8:1-9

But I'm not rich. I live on a missionary allowance. I've left most of my possessions, my bank account, and I'm living within the mission budget. I don't even have my own vehicle to drive. My house is simple— no carpets on the floor, no hot water, very few modern conveniences such as a telephone or electricity. No, can't you see I'm not a rich American?!

But, you have an expensive camera, wear different clothes every day, have a vehicle to drive and money to go on vacation or for plane tickets to go to the States. Your storeroom is full of food. You eat a good meal three times a day. Your house is "big"—individual bedrooms, running water, indoor plumbing. You must be rich!

What is our response to the accusation of being rich Americans? Do we deny it?

My father taught me a valuable lesson on one of his visits to us. Ansil had graciously done an errand for him, and Dad offered him a schilling. Ansil looked at him in amazement and said, "Pop, you must be rich!" Dad just quietly replied, "Yes, Ansil, I am rich." From that day on there was a special bond between them, and I never heard any more comments about Pop being rich!

135

We need to humbly confess we are rich and then seek ways to simplify our life-styles, learn to live like those around us, and do with less. Each person needs to find the area in his life that can be simplified. We are disciples as we leave all and follow Him. Jesus left the riches of His Father's house and experienced poverty so that He could feel with us in our poverty. Can we do less?

Disappointments

READ: II Thessalonians 3:1-5

I loved her. She was my sister in Christ. We did many things together. I thought she would remain faithful. She didn't.

He showed so much promise. We expected him to become a good church leader. What potential! But he, too, turned his back on Christ and the church.

Disappointments! It hurts us keenly when Christian brothers and sisters fall into sin. It's especially painful when they are our spiritual children. After repeated episodes of unfaithfulness in those we love, it becomes hard to love and trust again.

How do we handle our disappointment when converts backslide? Do we blame others and ourselves? Do we become discouraged? Do we avoid becoming attached to new Christians in order to protect ourselves in case they prove unfaithful? Or do we look to the One who will never disappoint us?

Paul, as a missionary, suffered many disappointments. Even so, he wrote to some of his followers, "But the Lord is faithful, who shall stablish you, and keep you from evil. And we have confidence in the Lord touching you, that ye both do and will do the things which we command you" (II Thessalonians 3:3, 4).

We, too, can have confidence in the Lord concerning those who trust in Him. Best of all, we can know that God is faithful. He promised never to leave us nor forsake us. He keeps His promises. We can be sure He'll never disappoint us.

CHAPTER SIX

"Come Into My House, and Abide There"

Acts 16:15

Entertain Angels

READ: Romans 12:13; I Peter 4:9; Hebrews 13:1, 2

Who, me, Lord—entertain angels?
But I'm not worthy to receive angels in my home.
Besides, our house is so small,
and it needs a good cleaning;
the beds are unmade, and the dishes aren't washed.
Just give me a few days or a week maybe to
get my house in order, or maybe
when the children are a little older and their
manners are better—I'd be ashamed, God, of
their behavior, their endless chatter.
You know it's not that I wouldn't want to entertain angels.
But I'm always busy; there are people at the door—
unexpected visitors; seems like I'm always
planning meals, preparing food for the many
extra people at the table, and I've become
tired and weary—but if You'll give me
a little time, I'll close my door to the visitors,
to the people who constantly want to talk or borrow
something, and I'll prepare my house for angels.
I'll clean every corner and prepare the best food
and dress the children in their Sunday best,
and we'll gladly welcome angels into our home!
Who, me, Lord? You say I have entertained angels!
What, those many strangers who have shared our
simple meals were angels?
Yes, my child, angels unaware, for as much as
ye have done it unto the least,
ye have done it unto ME!

140

Visitors, Visitors, Visitors

READ: I Peter 4:7-10

Mrs. Missionary had had a hard day. The house was full of visitors. Most of them had dropped in unexpectedly. She felt imposed upon. Was this what mission work was all about, running a free motel service?

Utterly weary, she was glad the beds were all made, the supper dishes washed, and breakfast half-planned. Soon everyone would go to bed and she'd be able to relax.

Then she heard the motor of an approaching car. It stopped by their door. A car door slammed. As Mrs. Missionary opened the door, her heart sank. More visitors! They were taking suitcases out of the taxi.

As they walked up to the door, Mrs. Missionary blurted, "What are we going to do? We're full."

Shocked by the unusual greeting, the visitors hired the taxi to take them to another mission station. Mrs. Missionary's reaction to their arrival colored their experience negatively. They never returned.

Another family visited the same mission on a different occasion. The missionaries received them cordially. With warmth and kindness, they made their guests feel at home. When this family left, they took good memories with them.

Years later, God called them to serve in the country

they had visited. They accepted the call. The memories of the positive experiences they'd had helped them make the decision. Now serving there, they say that a missionary's response to visitors can have a powerful influence.

I may be hosting persons whom the Lord will call to the mission field. How will my hospitality affect their response to God's call? My guests may be future missionaries. May that realization help me be a better hostess.

Use Hospitality One to Another

READ: Genesis 18:1-10

God's call to hospitality is clear, "Use hospitality one to another without grudging" (I Peter 4:9). God wants me to open my home cheerfully and lovingly, and gladly prepare meals for others and offer them a place to sleep.

Elsewhere the Scripture teaches, "Be kindly affectioned one to another with brotherly love . . . distributing to the necessity of saints; given to hospitality" (Romans 12:10a, 13).

Our homes should be open to strangers. "Let brotherly love continue. Be not forgetful to entertain strangers; for thereby some have entertained angels unawares" (Hebrews 13:1, 2).

An incident happened when I was about ten years old that has stuck with me. Our family was traveling in the western part of the United States when we met a hitchhiker traveling in the same direction. He stayed with us several days as we traveled across Utah and Nevada, sleeping in our car and eating meals with us at our trailer. We may never see that hitchhiker again, but Christ's love was portrayed to him as we shared what we had. Sharing one's hospitality is an excellent

143

way to reach our fellowman.

It is easy to be hospitable to those who would return the invitation. But in America we seldom invite the unsaved, out-of-our-class type of people. Instead it is our good friends, Grandpas, Uncle John, or Aunt Mary.

Abraham exercised hospitality when three men came to him. He did not have all of the modern conveniences we have today. Have you ever thought about how much work was involved in entertaining those angels? Abraham's actions illustrate the true meaning of hospitality. Let's exercise hospitality cheerfully one to another.

Company's Coming

READ: Genesis 18:1-8

Company's coming. The children are excited, and I groan within as I find myself thinking that the other company just left. The extra things that should be getting done are pushed aside once more. The sewing things will wait again; the patching pile is higher; and I hope the company won't notice the corners in the house that have been "rounded" to accommodate my overfull schedule.

I decided long ago that company is fed simple meals, but even so, it takes longer to fix twice as much as usual. And the children feel it, too, when we are extra busy with company.

Company comes. It's on our busiest day. We wouldn't have thought that we could manage all the unplanned-for things that came up. But company fixed the soup for supper, washed the dishes, helped us get to church on time.

Company comes, bringing encouragement we needed. Their enthusiasm and interest in the new things they hadn't seen or tasted before adds spice. Their wonder at the simple living is good for us.

Company comes. It's good to hear from "home" and of others we haven't seen or heard from for years. It is also good to meet new faces and form new friendships. We appreciate the thoughts they share in our services, bringing fresh courage and challenges to us.

Company leaves. We look at each other and smile. "Wasn't that nice they came!"

Unexpected Guests

READ: Genesis 18:1-8

It was almost bedtime. I felt a sense of satisfaction at having figured out where everyone would sleep. Our house seemed about to burst with visitors and Bible school teachers. Surely, I thought, we wouldn't have room for one more person.

Then we heard it, a shout at our gate. There it was again. Someone was calling my husband's name, in English.

Another overnight guest? we wondered. It was a vanload of them!

It's surprising what you can come up with when you think you're at the end of your resources. They say there's always room for one more. I learned that there's room even for one more vanload.

After greeting everyone and inviting them in, we visited awhile. Then I gathered up all our quilts, sheets, and blankets. Soon the house looked like a disaster zone with floor beds all over the place.

At last everyone was bedded down except my husband and me. But what would we sleep on? We had used all the bedding. Nothing clean remained.

Fortunately, the clothes hamper was full of dirty wash. Giggling, I made a nest. It was lumpy and smelly, but we slept on it.

146

That was many years ago, but ever since then, those visitors send us regular donations. Every time we receive a check from them, it reminds me of the night we slept on dirty wash. It also reminds me that we sometimes get unexpected blessings from unexpected visitors.

Abraham got unexpected company, too. He hurried to meet them. He begged them to stay. He served them his best food. After dinner, his unexpected guests gave him an unexpected blessing—the promise of a son.

Abraham's reaction to his unexpected guests challenges me. I want to learn from his example to be (1) more hospitable, (2) more attentive to my guests, and (3) more willing to share.

"Be not forgetful to entertain strangers; for thereby some have entertained angels unawares" (Hebrews 13:2).

Hospitality—Willing
or Grudging?
READ: II Kings 4:8-17

In the above passage, Elisha was shown kind hospitality by the Shunamite woman. She asked her husband to build a room so he could come and go as he pleased. Many of us are not fortunate enough to have a special place for guests, but God still commands us to be hospitable. We are not only to appear hospitable, but we need to have genuine hospitality (Hebrews 13:2; I Peter 4:9).

Following are ten questions which will help you to evaluate the quality of your hospitality.

1. Do my husband and children feel free to invite someone to our house, without me getting frustrated?

2. Am I willing to share our home with those who are unable to invite me back?

3. Do I feel I must make meals to impress my guests or for their bodily nutrition?

4. Can I substitute ingredients, if need be, without apologizing?

5. Can a large family enter my house feeling at ease, not needing to worry if someone would accidentally spill something?

6. Am I willing to invite a holiday guest who is not

part of the family—one who would have to spend the day alone?

7. Am I ashamed to serve a simple meal?

8. Can I change my plans for the day if someone phones and asks me to care for their children?

9. Does it upset me if someone stops in without notice?

10. If someone phones and seems to want to chat, or perhaps share a burden that is on her heart, do I cut her off abruptly, giving her the impression my work is more important than what is on her heart?

As friends and strangers alike cross the threshold of my house, may I remember each one has an eternal soul. My house doesn't. The food I serve to them doesn't. The little things I'd like to do for myself don't. May my intentions always honor God as I provide for the needs of my guests, whether it is washing dishes or lending a listening ear.

Getting in
"Pennsylvania Shape"

READ: Matthew 6:25-34

Company's coming from Pennsylvania, and I have only four more days to get ready! I feel a tremendous urge to have the house in "Pennsylvania shape." How will I get everything done in time?

I seem to hear Jesus saying, "Martha, Martha," but I don't have time to listen to Him. I'm busy scrubbing walls, mopping floors, and shaking dust cloths. My reputation is at stake.

But wait! Why am I trying to do the impossible? A house in El Salvador's dry season can't be compared with a house in Pennsylvania. The accumulation of dust that swirls into my house in one day is greater than a month's worth in Pennsylvania. Oh, what will these visitors think?

Does it matter what they think? Does it matter if my house is dirtier than theirs? Does it matter if they don't understand?

Yes, it does. I want to be understood, respected, and loved. Still, I'm beginning to see that some things are more important than the impressions I make on my visitors.

Eternal souls are more important than the

150

temporary state of my house.

Concern for my visitors' comfort and happiness is more important than concern about what they think of me.

My family's happiness is more important than making a good (probably false) impression on visitors.

Sitting at Jesus' feet is more important than cleaning and cooking.

Help me, Lord, to stop worrying and fretting about so many things. I want to choose, as Mary did, the better alternative, fellowship with You.

Visitors from Home

READ: Habakkuk 3:17-19; Psalm 84:11

Dear God, tonight our visitors are arriving on the bus. It's going to be a busy week. A lot of my morning devotions are going to be short. Late nights of catching up on home news make sleepy mornings. And it takes longer to make breakfast for visitors. So please help me to stay in tune with You as I cook and visit with our family.

Lord, I'm lonely. Our visitors left last night. Their visit was bodily evidence of their prayers for us when the day our house was full of brown visitors. This week I'll need Your Spirit's reminders for patience.

Thank You for the fellowship of kindred minds. It met my social needs. But they are gone, so here I come to You for fellowship.

While they were here, we lived for the joys of the week. Now we get back to the reality of our work. What do You want us to do here? What are Your directions for doing it?

Our good times together made me forget that sad spot in my heart. (How did You celebrate our baby's first birthday in heaven?) Now that the house is quieter, I am conscious how much I need Your grace to say no to depression and live thankfully.

Thank You, God for one very happy week. But thank You that when the activity and rapid-fire talking die down, You are still here. You are not just a visitor. You stay forever. Thank You.

Yes—With Thanks

READ: I Kings 17:8-24

Father,
did You say live-in guests for ten days?

Live-in guests mean
    more meals to fix,
    more dishes to wash,
    less time with my children,
    AND
    more opportunities to learn new things—
from recipes to methods of child training.

Live-in guests mean
    more laundry,
    more interruptions,   '
    less time with my husband,
    AND
    more enriching experiences for our children
(each individual You send brings his own ideas
and talents to share).

Live-in guests mean
    more sores and sickness to soothe,
    more questions to answer,
    less time with my local sisters and friends,
    AND
    more laughter.

Live-in guests mean
  more hours of work,
  less hours of rest,
  AND
  more refreshing fellowship.

Live-in guests mean
  the stripping off of "company manners" and being
  seen as we really are. (The thought of that can be
  scary!)
  AND
  the binding about us of family friends
  and pleasant memories.

Father, You make the "pluses" far outweigh the
"minuses." Yes, we'll take them, with thanks.

CHAPTER SEVEN

"Now Ye Also Put Off All These"

Colossians 3:8

Mudholes in Our Minds

READ: Philippians 4:4-8

It was a muddy, deeply rutted road we needed to take. The pickup coughed and sputtered as we climbed the first hill, then stalled at the top. We started the engine again, jerked through one mudhole, revved the motor and choked through another. As we viewed the worst spot ahead with its deep ruts, we knew if we didn't get through that place on the first try, we would be stuck.

We stopped. Together we prayed for safe passage through the mudhole. We were amazed, humbled, and deeply grateful as the pickup's coughing stopped and we slid through the ruts to the better road beyond.

How like our lives is that experience! We know the mudholes in our minds, those thoughts that are deep ruts we slide into and get high-centered on—fears of every kind, selfishness, unbelief, guilty feelings, doubts. We try to make it in our own strength, coughing, jerking, stalling, and getting nowhere. And then we stop at the end of ourselves and reach beyond ourselves to the Strength greater than ourselves.

We are amazed, humbled, and deeply grateful as we feel God's strength and leave the mudhole of depressing thoughts to come out victorious on the other side.

One More Night With the Frogs

READ: Psalm 42:1-5

I remember the late Menno J. Brunk, Th.D. That was the title of one of his sermons: "One more night with the frogs." Why, if frogs were stuck in bread dough and tangled in bed sheets, did Pharaoh say, "Intreat the Lord to take away the frogs *tomorrow*"? I would have pled for instant release.

A friend gave me a book for Christmas: *Sometimes I Prefer to Fuss*, by Vera Peets, a missionary in Thailand. That phrase pounces on me often. Some brown friends from another village come unexpectedly at mealtime. To them, it is an honor to serve us tortillas and fish in their home. To me, it is often a bother. I grumble. If God's grace is sufficient to be a gracious hostess, why am I grouchy? Because I prefer to be.

I shut myself in my room to cry over the photos of our sweet baby that died a year ago. After several days of this, the God of all comfort says, "Dry your tears." I say, "I want to cry more. Tears are healing."

It is healing to hide in God's strong arms and cry. The heart is much lighter if that heavy water is dumped out. But these tears made my heart water-logged and weightier. Some tears are healing. Some are not. If God comforts, why do I go on mourning? Because I prefer to.

Lord, forgive. Please take away the frogs right now.

157

Self-Pity: Justifiable?

READ: Psalm 40:1-8

He needs to be gone again for a week. How am I going to face another whole week alone with the children? They seem to know they can try things which they wouldn't normally try. I don't sleep as well, so of course my patience runs short. The chores—somehow we get through them, always taking longer than if he were here. Decisions—endless decisions I am not used to making by myself. People try to compensate by inviting us to have meals with them, which often makes things even more hectic. We take our places on Sunday morning with vague empty feelings because he is missing. The brotherhood is so kind, but that doesn't give me the security that his presence does. He is the glue that holds us all together, the oil that makes our home run smoothly.

Surely I can wade around the edge of the pond of self-pity, or perhaps an invigorating dive would be permissible for someone who has sacrificed all that I have. Just as I am ready to take the plunge, I'm reminded of the encouraging words of a sister the day my husband was ordained. She said, "Be thankful your husband is qualified for the work of the ministry." I am also reminded of the four widows in our group who spend countless hours by themselves. I

158

also know of several sisters whose husbands have left them for another or for the fleeting pleasures of sin.

Pity—how can I pity myself when I have been so blessed? I want to use this opportunity to remember to intercede in the behalf of those whose husbands have been called Home, and try harder to understand their needs. I must remember to pray for those whose husbands have turned their back on the Lord and do what I can to brighten their dark and dreary days. No, self-pity is not justifiable.

The Choice Is Mine

READ: I Kings 19

Oh, that sneaky, subtle sin of self-pity! What a comfortable blanket to wrap yourself in when you've been disappointed. "There's nothing I can do about it; I am being used; poor little me; I am just a victim of circumstances." Have you ever felt that way? Maybe you've heard yourself saying, "I never know what to expect. I can never tell when my husbaand will be home . . . or when he'll be in for supper . . . or when the next visitors will come."

No doubt women are more prone to self-pity than men. Maybe we have more reasons for it! But Elijah was one man who felt sorry for himself and became very depressed. After the great victory on Mt. Carmel, he had a real "down" and ran for the wilderness. He thought he was all alone, but God knew where he was. God sent an angel to provide food for Elijah, and then He let him sleep awhile. A bit later God said, "Go, return . . ." (I Kings 19:15).

When we sense the clouds of self-pity surrounding us, we too need to remember that God knows where we are and understands our circumstances. But instead of blaming others, we should ask, "What can *I* do to make the most of this situation?" We have a built-in, God-given creativity which we need to employ in service to others, especially when we are being tempted to focus on ourselves. If you often find yourself waiting for people, make use of that time with constructive activity. Sometimes self-pity creeps in when we are lonely. What better antidote than to reach out to other lonely and needy people! Self-pity can also strike when we are overloaded with work and activities. Maybe you can solicit help or determine how you can simplify your work.

Perhaps the best way to overcome self-pity is to choose to accept the particular situation rather than fight it or passively shrink under it. Then we are no longer victims but free to act in a constructive way.

Self-Pity Creed

READ: Numbers 11:10-15

Because I struggled so much with self-pity, I decided I needed a "creed." I came up with three basic truths about self-pity and how I should respond to it based on God's principles.

1. I believe that self-pity is, at heart, rebellion against God and His plan for me. As such it is a sin classed with witchcraft (I Samuel 15:23). (Is that too strong?)

2. I believe that every situation and every detail of every situation is designed or allowed by a loving Father with my good in mind. Because this is true, I will not blame other people for what comes into my experience (Jeremiah 29:11). (Sometimes when I look for someone to blame, I realize God was the *only One* who could have arranged anything different, and He didn't, so it must be right.)

3. Whenever a situation tempts me to self-pity, I commit myself to view that situation as a test. If I pass the test, I grow. If I fail, I will need to repeat the test sometime (James 1:2, 3).

God's Crop

READ: Romans 12:17-21

A certain farmer in western Canada was getting his machinery ready to harvest his annual crop of wheat. Suddenly dark clouds rose in the sky and within thirty minutes a monstrous hailstorm destroyed 80 percent of his crop. His friend asked him if he wasn't terribly upset at this tremendous loss. He replied, "For about two minutes I forgot whose crop it was. Then I remembered I had given it to the Lord. I decided if that's what He wants to do with His crop, it's all right, and I'm sure He has another way to look after me."

When a natural catastrophe happens, we can sometimes accept it by labeling it "an act of God." But what about the times when people are involved in destroying our possessions?

When we first moved to Hudson, the local people told us we wouldn't be able to have a garden. "The neighbor children," they said, "will just raid your garden and you won't have anything anyway."

But every year we plant a garden. And every year someone pulls out carrots from the time they are half-grown or picks raspberries as soon as they ripen. Usually it happens after dark or when we are away.

I was especially upset the year they pulled up several prized cabbage heads and threw them across the fence into another yard. Then I thought of the verse. "Vengeance is mine; I will repay, saith the Lord" (Romans 12:19). My quick response was "Oh, please, Lord, don't be too hard on them. It's only garden produce!"

I want to learn to hold lightly to "our" earthly possessions and remember to whom they really belong. I also pray for love and wisdom to respond in the right way to each situation.

Kitchen Offerings

READ: Matthew 6:1-4

Sacrifice: destruction or surrender of something valued or desired for the sake of a higher object or more pressing claim.

That's the dictionary definition. We mothers can identify with it. There are the situations such as the dish the native maid broke and we said little about it for the sake of her feelings, or the last onion in the bag sold to a sister to keep good relationships. We experience them daily—these little "kitchen offerings." We know how much they cost.

Sometimes I enjoyed the sense of righteousness I felt when telling someone else about my sacrifices. It was a pleasant feeling to know that they knew how much I was giving up.

Then one day after making another "offering" and then talking about it, the Spirit prodded my conscience. Searchingly He asked, "How pleased is the Lord with a sacrifice gone public?" I began to wonder. I looked at the great Example. Jesus Himself spoke little about what He sacrificed to be our Saviour. It was others who pointed out what He gave up and suffered.

To stand my sacrifices beside His one great sacrifice made mine seem quite trivial—indeed, hardly worth talking about at all, let alone bragging on them.

"But sometimes we have to talk to someone!" the weary mother-heart cries. Oh, isn't that true? The very frequency of these offerings can make them into a routine that drags down our spirits. Despite our determination to be cheerful, we begin to feel sapped. Talking to someone who understands can be a wonderful tonic for tired nerves.

And now, I'm finally coming to realize the truth the Lord wants me to share. A lot depends on what *reason* I have for talking about my sacrifices.

Thank You, Lord, for showing this to me. I need to go check out my motives.

Giving Grudgingly

READ: I Corinthians 4:7-9; I Timothy 3:8-13

I know I shouldn't have been so inhospitable, so reluctant. I should have been happy to feed the man's belly and been willing to please my husband by honoring the invitation.

But why didn't my husband ask me first if it was all right with me? Or if I had enough food? And when I did put a portion on his plate, my husband piled on more. The man from the next village could've gone to one of his relatives. There are plenty of them in this village. And his immediate response to everything we said about Christ was, "That's true." Every time. Then why did he give up believing? And why did he talk about starting a believers' church in his village "when God tells me to"—and then several hours later walk down the river to the *che-che* (home-brew) pot?

Besides, I'm not feeling well enough to be confronted with this situation now . . .

My child, are you any more My creation than he? I love him and see him as a potential child of Mine—a believer, a new creature. I see a hungry heart—unhappy, in a deep hole, unable to find his way out.

The food? Wouldn't you be hungry after walking through the jungle one-and-a-half hours? What do you

167

have that you didn't receive? And who has been the Giver?

Submit to your husband and willingly open your home to others. I'll honor you if you honor your husband. Release him for usefulness in kingdom ministries. Give him the freedom to hand over a plate of food—and to pile on more. Give him the freedom to minister to the people I've called you both to.

Do him good and not evil all your days. And his heart will safely trust in you. He will praise you.

Then stretch out your hands to the poor. Reach forth your hands to the needy. And I will clothe you with strength and honour. You will rejoice in time to come . . .

Be secure in Me.

Hospitality Without Hypocrisy

READ: Romans 6:4-11

Another visitor at the door! I struggle with hypocrisy. A Christian should be truthful. Should I just let her know I am not glad to see her?

Show mercy with cheerfulness. But right now I don't *feel* cheerful. Should I just be a hypocrite and pretend?

It is not hypocritical to believe the *fact* that God's love is working in me; to ignore, no, crucify the *feeling* that there is no more love left.

"Knowing this, that our old man [impatience] is crucified with him [every unhandy time someone comes to the door], that the body of sin [impatience] might be destroyed, that henceforth we should not serve sin [the *feeling* that we ran out of love]. . . . Now if we be dead with Christ [to our feelings], we believe that we shall also live with him [in the *fact* of His love working in us as we cheerfully show hospitality]" (Romans 6:6, 8).

Now go meet the visitor at the door!

Respect of Persons

READ: James 2:1-9

I read a story to my daughter about a man who had been invited to a feast at a good friend's house. He had been working in his fields all day and had no time to go home and change into his good clothes. He just washed up at the river and hurried to his friend's house, hoping to get there before the feast began. He was on time, but his friend ignored him even when he spoke to him. The host seated all his finely dressed guests at a table laden with food. The man in his work clothes was still ignored. At last he ran home and changed into his best clothing and returned to the feast. This time he was welcomed with open arms. After being seated, he began to put food into his pockets saying "Eat, coat, eat." The host questioned his behavior. He explained that since he had been ignored in his work clothes but was received graciously when he was well-dressed, it had to be the clothes that were wanted at the feast and not his person.

While explaining this to Susana, I wondered if I was guilty of this. I graciously received Emiliana into my home whenever she knocked on my door. She was careful to wipe the mud from her shoes before she entered and was generally a well-groomed sister. But what of poor _____, who was dirty and unkempt? Was she welcomed the same even though I knew I would need to sweep the floor after she left?

God is not a respecter of persons, and I have no excuse to be either.

Anger

READ: Jonah 4

Some Kekchi customs are aggravating. Some make me angry. (Rooting pigs on the loose!)

I feel safe calling it anger, because I am surrounded by modern psychologists who encourage us to express our feelings. My husband is more old-fashioned. He calls anger sin. James agrees: "The wrath of man worketh not the righteousness of God" (James 1:20).

I thought some anger to be healthy. It moves us from indifference to action. Jesus was angry at the Pharisees. He was displeased with the disciples for turning away the children. And what does "Be ye angry, and sin not" mean?

With concordance to defend me, I searched the lists under "anger." Most Scriptures were from the Old Testament, concerning God's wrath on sin. Why would I choose to live there, when Christ offers me mercy and grace?

Some anger is suicidal. When Jonah said, "It is better for me to die," God called that anger.

In the New Testament, *orge* (Greek) is slow-simmering. *Thumos* is quick to explode and subside. Both are sin. Both reveal areas unsurrendered to God. Destructive anger power can be transformed to constructive love power when surrendered.

I closed the concordances and Bible, my anger rebuked, not justified. Humanism wants me to coddle it. Jesus wants to cleanse it by His blood. Now I yield my excuses to the conquering power of the Lord Jesus.

171

Fear Dispelled

READ: Isaiah 41:8-14

My worst fears were coming true.

All during my pregnancy, I had lived with insecurity because of increased political turmoil and violence. Other missionaries had left El Salvador. I was scared.

What would happen if I couldn't get to the hospital? Who would stay with our children if I could? Would it be safe to drive to the hospital?

Five days before my due date, we could hear bomb blasts from Santa Ana. The war had officially started. A dusk-to-dawn curfew made it easy to decide where we'd have the baby.

God filled me with a deep sense of peace and confidence. For several days, He even took away my fear. With new courage, I prepared for a home delivery.

On January 19, 1981, Paul Andrew was born with only my husband and God in attendance. What a priceless experience! Best of all, the warmth of God's love enfolded us, dispelling the chill of fear.

Isaiah 41:10: "Fear thou not; for I am with thee: be not dismayed; for I am thy God: I will strengthen thee; yea, I will help thee; yea, I will uphold thee with the right hand of my righteousness."

Don't Procrastinate

READ: Proverbs 3:27-35

The tendency to put things off is common to all. It is not always a sin to procrastinate. It becomes sin when it hinders God's work. We are "devising evil against our neighbor" when we procrastinate. To overcome this tendency, we need to remember life's priorities and decide to do something about them *now*. We do not postpone matters which we consider really important.

On Christmas Eve our family went caroling for several non-Christian neighbors in town. After we finished singing at the Matter's home, Mrs. Matter accused me of never visiting. It was true, I had good intentions to visit her, but my priorities were not correct. Mrs. Matter is not a Christian, and I had missed many good opportunities to witness.

It is our God-ordained duty to do good. "For we are his workmanship, created in Christ Jesus unto good works, which God hath before ordained that we should walk in them" (Ephesians 2:10). We are all capable of doing good. "It is in the power of thine hand to do it," Solomon says (Proverbs 3:27b). Being busy does not excuse us. If the Holy Spirit has impressed upon you the need to write a letter, visit the sick, or witness to someone, don't procrastinate!

Learn with me to use the technique of "prioritizing" each day. List your duties and opportunities in order of importance. Then take up the most important thing first and get at it immediately. Don't procrastinate!

Javelin of Jealousy

READ: I Samuel 18:1-9

The javelin of jealousy did you say? Oh, no, surely not among missionary wives.

And why not? Where can you find more vulnerable hearts to jab?

Opportunities are plentiful.

There are opportunities to be jealous of possessions. Why did *she* get the new stove? Her family always sends her so many goodies. Why can't *I* live in a house with a varnished board floor?

There are opportunities to be jealous of privileges. She just went to the city last month. She entertains visitors from "home" so often.

There are opportunities to be jealous of personal relations. Her husband stays home much more than mine. Why does Sister A *always* confide in her?

Praise, performance, poise, and productivity all present their peculiar opportunities.

What do I do when I discover that I have had a javelin in my hand? I must confess it as the wicked sin it is. I must accept the uniqueness of people—God has fitted each of us where He wants us for the growth of His kingdom. I must tell my sister the good I see in her.

Let me remember this in time to come.

174

How to Stop Criticism

READ: Ephesians 4:25-32

Speaking evil of another is destructive to the body of Christ. It tears apart and divides. It is little wonder then that the Bible commands, "Put them in mind to . . . speak evil of no man, to be no brawlers, but gentle, showing all meekness unto all men" (Titus 3:1, 2).

People who constantly criticize others and delight in speaking evil of them reveal a poor self-image and weakness of character. By contrast, those who delight in praising others, focusing on their good points and passing along good reports about them, reflect a proper self-image and a kind, loving heart. By commending others, they discourage unkind remarks from others. Instead of tearing down, they build up.

Two boys on the school playground were discussing a classmate. One of them remarked, "He's no good at sports."

The other quickly responded, "Yes, but he always plays fair."

"He isn't very smart in school either," the critical one added.

His friend answered, "That may be true, but he studies hard."

The boy with the mean tongue was becoming

175

exasperated with the attitude of the other. "Well," he sneered, "did you ever notice how ragged his clothes are?"

The other boy kindly replied, "Yes, but did you ever notice, they're always clean!"

Every unkind observation was countered by a kind one. What a wonderful way to stop criticism! Let us refrain from evil speaking and be "kind one to another." Rather than contributing to the spirit of criticism, let us be known as those who cancel it.

A Critical Spirit

READ: Psalm 51

Lord, I've been so critical. It seems no one does anything the way I think they should. I criticize the children for the way they eat. I send them back to the bathroom to wash again. I am constantly reminding them to pick up after themselves. As my husband steps into the kitchen to take a phone call, I eye his muddy boots with contempt. When a sister phones and asks me to help her butcher chickens, I wonder why she couldn't have asked someone who isn't so busy. I think of the faults of others and wonder why they can't see them as well as I can.

Yes, Lord, I've been critical again. Help me to be more tolerant of the children when they need to be reminded to do better. I must remember how often You need to remind me to examine the corners of my mind to see why I become critical and short-tempered. As I clean up my husband's muddy tracks, help me to use this opportunity to say, "Thank You, Lord. I'm so grateful for a kind, loving husband who so diligently serves You." If someone helps me change my plans, I need to remember that You must plan my day, thanking You for the opportunity to fellowship with another sister. Please help me to consider others' faults as needs which may soon pass away as I lift them to the throne of grace.

Forgive me for my critical spirit. Thank You for showing me *my* needs and for being patient with *my* faults.

Of Mixers and Treasures

READ: Matthew 6:19-24

I have a mixer. A "KitchenAid" mixer. It's a good one, and with all the people who eat at our table, I use it constantly. My husband gave it to me for Christmas the year before we came to the mission field, and I was delighted! After much debate, we brought it along, and it has been used plenty.

The last while there have been a lot of break-ins and stealing on the compound. In fact, last evening a thief broke into our house. He took a pie, a box of cornflakes, some eggs, and the change drawer. (Apparently he was hungry.) But . . . did he not see the mixer? Maybe he had his hands so full he couldn't carry it and has plans of coming back for it. He can have just about anything in this house but that mixer. The tape recorder and tapes are replaceable and not of sentimental value. We don't have money, and besides, money would be replaceable. He wouldn't want our clothes. I can't think of anything else he'd want except that mixer. He could sell it and make himself a small dollar.

But wait. I hear the Lord speaking! "Are you laying up treasures in heaven or on earth? If that silly little mixer is your treasure then THAT is where your heart is!"

Oh, what a foolish place to have my heart. "Lord, thank You for this painful reminder to have the right kind of treasures."

Of Garbage and Grapevines

READ: James 3:1-12

As I stepped out the door and headed for the garbage pile, I heard running footsteps approaching. Village dogs, trained by past experience, came hurrying for their share of our refuse. I quite despised them—they were so scrawny and eager for trash. Yet regardless of my opinion of them, they continued scavenging for our throwaways.

Later I wondered if I was like the dogs. Every village has its grapevine. Ours had one too. All you had to do was notice the village policeman walking past at six in the morning to know that there was probably something interesting going on. I came to enjoy finding out the trouble and passing it on. After all, it was only village unbelievers. There was nothing wrong with that, was there? Was there? Wasn't that gossip? Wasn't gossip despised in God's sight, regardless of who it was about or how true it was?

The answer, of course, is yes. Paul wrote, "Charity . . . rejoiceth not in iniquity" (I Corinthians 13:4a, 6). He made no distinction between brother or unbeliever. Any report of iniquity, particularly by way of the grapevine, needs to stop with me.

Eternal Exchange

READ: Matthew 16:21-28

What shall I give in exchange for my soul? The words ring in my ears as I think of many who are selling their souls for something so cheap. Things we wouldn't think of dabbling in—being a career woman, worldly entertainment, or the fashions of the world. But what did Jesus mean for me personally when He said these words? Would I exchange my soul for family, friends, bountiful and tasty meals, or recreation? Does eternity in heaven mean so little to me that I would exchange it for a nice house or good health? How about the peer pressure of others getting "x" amount accomplished and me merely spinning my wheels? Ah! now I'm getting closer home. I must remember that eternal accomplishments aren't usually visible.

Lord, today I want to concentrate on doing those things which count for eternity. Not just those things which I can show my friends and say, "See, look what I did," but rather things that maybe aren't much to show for. It may be just the lightening of a heavy heart, the drying of a child's tear, or perhaps just listening to someone who needs someone to talk to. And surely it includes cheerfully meeting the physical needs of those whose care has been entrusted to me.

Judging Ignorantly

READ: Romans 14:1-4, 14, 19

How many times have I ignorantly judged someone's behavior without knowing all the facts surrounding the circumstances? Far too many.

"What does _____ do with all his time?" This came from a visitor at a Central American mission.

"What do you mean?"

"Well, it appears to me as if _____ doesn't do enough visiting in the natives' homes, so I wondered what he did with all his time."

What an injustice to the missionary! Anyone who has never been a missionary does not have a complete idea what all a mission worker has on him.

Here is a sampling. The missionary has his family's welfare to look after. The marketing must be done periodically. Two or three messages per week must be prepared (often in a foreign language). Instruction classes take time. The emergency trips must be made to a doctor whenever someone gets sick or hurt. There are daily interruptions by those just passing by. Of course, what visitation can be done is also squeezed into this busy schedule.

Need I go on? The point has been made. Let us know all the facts before we judge. Like the old Indian proverb: "Don't judge another brave until you have walked a mile in his moccasins."

Thou That Judgest

READ: Romans 2:1-4

Impatience! I couldn't handle it, especially when it was flung at me. In younger years I learned to try my best to be punctual and undemanding and to avoid imposing on others. I hated when people became upset and impatient with me.

Even when impatience was not directed at me, I cringed. When I heard hasty unkindness thrown at someone else, I hurt for them. Perhaps at times it hurt me more than the actual receiver, who may have been used to it.

One day, it became my pleasure to be a mother. We loved our little daughter though many times we were frustrated in knowing how to care for an extra-fussy baby. Of course as an infant she was not responsible for the way she responded to her world, and we didn't expect her to be either.

But as she grew older, she did become responsible. Of course only in a small way at first. I think maybe I was expecting more of her than she was capable of. Or else I was not giving her enough loving guidance and discipline.

One day as a result of frustrated feelings over her irresponsibility, I discovered I was talking to her with hasty unkindness. What! I who hated and feared

182

impatience was now not the recipient but the giver of it.

My daughter gave no indication that I could see that she feared impatience as much as her mother did. But I wondered what deep and lasting impressions might already have been made on her tender soul.

I hope I won't forget this little lesson. And I wonder how many other faults there are that I despise in other folks but excuse and tolerate in myself.

Let us as mothers accept the challenge to examine ourselves honestly. Habits, thought patterns, responses to others—how do our own line up with what we expect of others? More importantly, how do we line up with the standard God has set for us?

Out of the Shadow, Part I

READ: Psalm 143

Discouragement, despondency, and depression used my house for a hangout. They entered without knocking or asking permission. And while depression held the door open, self-pity slipped in behind it like a shadow. Once inside, the dark threesome with the even darker shadow made themselves at home as though they planned to stay.

We've all had times like that, haven't we? Sometimes our depression is caused by physical problems. Then it's important to do what we can to correct the cause.

Probably more often we "get down" by circumstances beyond our control. We let our minds run away with us in imagining, reasoning, or just plain thinking.

Sometimes we find a perverse enjoyment in being depressed and in feeling sorry for ourselves. There is a black (if doubtful) comfort in seeing how far down we are and what has brought us there.

Then there are other times when we long desperately to rise but we feel powerless. Depression has fastened its iron grip on us and we think we can do nothing.

But there is a way! I wrestled long with it (sometimes not even wrestling, just giving in to it!), and I learned some important lessons during those dark days.

I couldn't get out of the shadow until I *wanted* to. Ask God to put His desire in you to stand tall and free of the shadow of self-pity.

Out of the Shadow, Part II

READ: Psalm 69:29-36

Years ago I had marked Psalm 69:30 in my Bible as the antidote for despondency. It continues to be God's cure. Singing when you don't feel like it can be a real sacrifice. Is that why the Hebrew writer calls it "the sacrifice of praise"? But singing is an important step out of the Shadow. Even if the tears run down our cheeks as we sing. Even if our voice wants to crack into a sob instead of staying on tune. Sing!

Another step out is to accept your circumstances. Believe that they are God's will for you. This is difficult, especially when other people are contributing to the unpleasantness around you. But it is important and it is a step out.

A thought that goes alongside this truth is one I learned from a booklet. *Looking Unto Jesus* emphasized that quote from Hebrews. Let's look to Jesus and not at ourselves, our feelings, our work, or our surroundings.

Philippians 4:8 gives us yet another step out. Replace those dark, brooding thoughts with better ones. In place of despair, discouragement, and doubt, think of things true, honest, just, pure, lovely, and of good report. Doing so lights a lamp in the Shadow.

One evening I was feeling so dark I wondered if I

185

was getting mentally sick. I shared my feelings with my husband. He suggested I try reading Psalm 23 thoughtfully five times a day for one week as prescribed in the book *God's Psychiatry.* I did this and it, too, proved to be a step out.

Sometimes, however, nothing helps; we are completely powerless. Then, Dear Sister, let us fall on God's grace, confessing that we are utterly helpless without Him. Let us trust Him to send the Light of Life into our lives again. That Light will melt the Shadow.

Praise His name for Jesus!

A Way of Escape

READ: Hebrews 4:12-16

Today was one of those days when all seemed to go wrong. It started out as usual and on schedule, but by the time breakfast was over the troubles began. Our second child took every excuse to cry, and the baby, who seemed tired, wouldn't sleep. It started raining after I had hung out three loads of wash. And the baby was fussing more, so I sat down and rocked her awhile. She had just gone to sleep when her wailing brother entered the room. Thankfully, the baby didn't waken, and I put her in bed to find out that my son's problem was the arrival of the health nurse. She kindly said she'd come again next month. I hurried to finish the wash with a wringer that wasn't working right. With my husband's help, dinner was ready on time for the teachers, but that still didn't help my rather unpleasant mood. All morning my thoughts had been whirling, quick prayers for strength and depressed feelings going round and round. I had tried to be grateful that I was healthy, and the next moment I was upset about something else. I thought about Romans 8:28 and realized that maybe patience was what this was all about, but I felt impatient with my circumstances today. When one of the teachers mentioned a problem she had had in school that morning,

187

I realized that I had not claimed the promise of I Corinthians 10:13 that morning:

"There hath no temptation taken you but such as is common to man: but God is faithful, who will not suffer you to be tempted above that ye are able; but will with the temptation also make a way to escape, that ye may be able to bear it" (I Corinthians 10:13).

We are not promised escape "from" the circumstances (as I was wishing for) but rather, escape "in" them, "that ye may be able to bear it."

CHAPTER EIGHT

Whose Adorning Let It Be of the Heart
I Peter 3:3, 4

The Fruit of the Spirit

READ: Galatians 5:22-26

But the fruit of the Spirit is—

LOVE: Lord, give me love for the unlovely—the beggar on the street, the village children at the door, those who take advantage of me, the one who spreads an evil report about me or my husband. You love them and I want to also!

JOY: Joy in spite of the circumstances around us, when it rains and rains and we've run out of clean clothes. Joy when our day is all planned and we get unexpected guests. Joy in knowing You are in control!

PEACE: Peace in the midst of the storm when the motor stalls and water and mud are on every side. Peace, not when all is going well, but when life is at its worst!

LONGSUFFERING: The same people, the same problems, often the same burdens—teach us to suffer long!

GENTLENESS: Jesus, You were gentle with the children, with those who had physical and spiritual needs—give me of your compassion!

GOODNESS: Rich in good works, helping those who are hungry, visiting those in prison, ministering to the needs of others!

FAITH: As a grain of mustard seed, not the amount

of faith, but the object of it—faith in a great God!

MEEKNESS: Willingness to help the other person up the ladder ahead of me—teach me to be a servant!

TEMPERANCE: Discipline to study Your Word, using my time wisely, spending my money or the mission's money in a way that will bring the most benefit to Your kingdom!

God, I realize I can't choose only part of this fruit to be evident in my life. I need the complete fruit of the Spirit, so that others may see Jesus in me.

Missionary Substitutions

READ: I Corinthians 13

Let's face it. Many things you used in the States aren't available or are too expensive. But for almost anything there is a substitute.

You can serve granola instead of Cheerios, powdered milk instead of fresh cow's milk, young field corn instead of sweet corn. You can substitute tortillas for bread, rice for potatoes, and cabbage for lettuce.

But there's no substitute for love.

You can make imitation maple syrup by boiling together two cups of sugar with one cup water. Add a few drops of maple flavoring. It tastes almost like the real thing.

But there's no substitute for love.

Cornflakes tossed with taco seasoning and melted butter, then toasted in an oven make passable taco chips. Three tablespoons of cocoa plus one tablespoon of butter equals one square of unsweetened chocolate. Mangoes and papayas can take the place of peaches and apples.

But there's no substitute for love.

You're out of spot remover? Try solar power. Soap up the stain. Spread the sudsy garment flat in direct sunlight. This is very effective.

But there's no substitute for love.

You don't have canned cream soups for preparing casseroles? Make a thick white sauce and vary the flavor by adding cheese, chopped onions, or celery, or by using broth instead of milk.

But there's no substitute for love.

For brown sugar, mix one cup of granulated sugar with two tablespoons of molasses. Natural cane sugar boiled with water takes the place of molasses.

But there's no substitute for love.

Lord, help me not to complain about the things that aren't available to me. Let me count my blessings and use creatively the resources I do have. Thank You for love, for which there is no substitute.

The Joy of Housekeeping
READ: Ecclesiastes 9:7-10

Is there really any joy in housekeeping, in the ordinary, everyday work that needs to be done—washing dishes, sweeping the floor, doing laundry? Our attitudes may have a lot to do with the joy we find in our daily work.

We are not just housekeepers but also homemakers! We are not just caring for a house but making a home! That home may find us in another country, far away from the comforts we've been familiar with, and we'll need to find joy right there in that corner of God's world!

Acceptance may be the key to joy—accepting our role as a wife and mother, accepting our home whether it's a thatch roof in the jungle or the mission headquarters with a constant stream of visitors!

We need to accept the daily routine of life, the endless work waiting to be done! A pleasant atmosphere in a clean home makes others feel comfortable. The more complicated our living, the more work is necessary to keep it clean. Let's keep our homes simple and avoid the clutter of unnecessary accumulation.

Make your home attractive. Be creative. Creativity is free! A few plants (they're free for your finding in the bush, if you're fortunate enough to live in the jungle), pictures on the wall, a bowl of attractively arranged fruits or vegetables; these can make your home a special place.

Be sure that your family, your co-workers, and the nationals sense that you love your home and that you are happy right where God has placed you!
JOY IS CONTAGIOUS!

194

Mommy, Sing!
READ: Psalm 96

"Sing, Mommy, sing," my two little ones often say. If I kept up with their urgings, I would be perpetually in song.

Would that be so bad? Reviewing my past, I realized there was a time when I often sang while working. Somehow I lost the habit, and Satan has tried to fill the void with irritableness. If I had been singing, I know the children's little mistakes and clumsiness would not have bothered me so much.

I tried an experiment. I began to sing again while going about my daily duties. It worked. Life became much more pleasant. My nerves were calmer, and the children even behaved better!

Now whenever they beg for me to sing, I try to squelch the desire to say, "I don't feel like it." I know things go much more smoothly when I sing.

195

A Touch

READ: Colossians 3:12-17

A touch—

Babies need a mother's touch. A baby left in a crib without physical contact will die—it needs to be loved and cuddled.

Children need a touch to soothe their hurts and bumps. They need a good-night kiss and tender loving care!

Teenagers need a touch, a hug when their world seems upside down and no one really understands.

Wives need a touch, a clasp of the hand, a husband's encircling arms when the going gets rough.

Husbands need a touch, to show appreciation for their hard work, their love, and support!

Our friends need a touch, a hand on the shoulder when they're hurting. They need to hear us say, "I care about you, I love you, and I want to do what I can to make it easier for you." Or at times they may need a touch without words, just letting them know we're there. We may not know what to say, but we can show we care about what is happening in their lives and we're ready to help when they need us!

A touch can release those pent-up feelings, can produce a flood of tears that will bring healing to damaged emotions. A touch involves us personally in another person's life. We make their hurts become our concerns. God cares about us. He sent His Son to touch our lives and to bring healing and peace to us, and we in turn are the instruments of His peace.

But I Need Patience, NOW!

READ: Romans 5:1-5

In my search for patience, I discovered the formula for gaining patience in Romans 5:3: "We glory in tribulations also: knowing that tribulation worketh patience." Here is the formula: PRESSURE PRODUCES PATIENCE.

How many times have I prayed for patience and expected it instantly? God has given opportunities to cultivate patience, and I have not recognized them.

An opportunity came while I was waiting on my minister-husband to go home from church. The minutes were ticking by and the pressure was mounting to complain about the lateness of the hour.

Or, on another occasion, we had a special evening planned and our family was ready to leave. Then the phone rang and my doctor-husband had to go to deliver a baby. Here was another opportunity to develop patience as I learned to accept the frustrations of having our plans changed.

Motherhood has given many opportunities to gain patience: the numerous questions, countless interruptions, cleaning up all those messes—and the list could go on. All these demands have and are producing patience in me.

James told us to "let patience have her perfect work" (James 1:4) so that we could be complete, not lacking anything. When I am tempted to be impatient, I need to pray for strength and thank the Lord for another opportunity to learn patience.

Patience Is a Gem

READ: James 1:2-4; 5:7-11

She came to me in all her sweet four-year-old innocence and asked, "Mommy, is there anything you need?"

"Yes, I need patience," I answered immediately.

"Okay," she responded, "I'm going to town on my motorcycle and I'll bring you some."

Her little feet pattered down the steps and presently she revved up her tricycle.

Soon she was back with a block of wood informing me, "This is the Daddy Patience, and I'll be back later with the Mama and Baby."

Wooden blocks are easily acquired, sawed, burned, or pounded into pieces. Patience is a gem, not a wooden block.

Some precious gems are formed in deep waters, some in violent heat or pressure, and others in arid places. They are made lovely by careful, consistent cutting and polishing with hard abrasives. The *World Book Encyclopedia* says, "Like tiny buds that burst into beautiful blossom, dull lumps of mineral matter can be cut and polished into brilliantly flashing or beautifully glowing gems."

The trying of my faith, under my loving heavenly Father's control, fashions in me through abrasive circumstances the gem of patience.

Never Give Up!

READ: Philippians 1:1-11

While putting the finishing touches on a quilt that had been started nearly four years earlier, I was contemplating the rewards of perseverance. The quilt was called "Broken Star" and had many small diamonds sewn together. I had had to work at it with many interruptions. It seemed I would never finish, but I kept plugging away, envisioning a beautiful quilt on our bed.

Perseverance pays in gardening, too. During the hot summer I wonder, "Is it really worth it?" Pulling weeds in the strawberry bed is certainly not my "cup of tea"! But the rewards are great when I pop those juicy berries into my mouth.

The Apostle Paul persevered in prayer day and night while in prison. He wrote again and again assuring others of his prayers on their behalf and requesting that others pray for him.

Our congregation persevered in prayer a number of years for a family that attended our church. The husband and wife had marital problems and the children were rebellious. It seemed that our efforts to help were in vain. I was tempted to quit praying.

But all of a sudden things began to happen! The daughter began to realize that a life of sin is not easy. During our fall revival meetings this family made new commitments to the Lord. My faith was strengthened as I realized again the rewards of perseverance in prayer. Never give up!

199

It Wasn't So Bad After All

READ: Romans 16:1, 2, 6, 12

I dreaded that trip! How could I keep three active boys happy in our tiny Subaru for a week? Traveling to Central America had been fun for us before, but this time was different. Six months pregnant, I felt unable to cope with the challenge of making this trip an interesting event for my family. Worse, I was afraid to go home to El Salvador. We had left because of danger to my husband. Now his strong sense of duty was calling him back to the land of our hearts. I packed listlessly, apprehensive about the upcoming journey.

The evening before our departure a former classmate brought a boxful of mysterious-looking parcels. "You may open one every day of your trip," she told our wide-eyed boys.

How exciting! The boys could hardly wait to start. Soon I was almost eager to go in spite of myself.

Taking turns to unwrap the gifts, we found:
— Travel games
— Coloring books and crayons
— Toys
— Notes assuring us of love and prayers
— Towels and washcloths
— Snacks
— Storybooks

200

— A jar of home-canned vegetable soup
— A self-addressed AIRFORM
— Notebooks, pens, and pencils

The week-long car trip turned out to be less difficult than I had feared. Those little gifts helped so much. I wondered at the thoughtfulness that had inspired them. Why had a casual acquaintance been so kind? How could she have understood my needs so well? I believe she must have allowed God to work through her.

Even now, years later, the memory of her kindness makes me want to be more sensitive to the needs of others.

Oh, Lord, thank You for the kindness You show to me through others. Help me share Your kindness, too.

Faith

READ: Hebrews 11:1-10

Faith. What is it? One of the best answers is found in Hebrews, but I also like what Webster's states, "Unquestioning belief, specifically in God; complete trust or confidence."

How can I apply faith to my life as Abraham of old did? Do I really mean it whenever I ask God to increase my faith? Often I am afraid to ask for more faith because I dread the consequences. I am afraid God will ask something of me that I am not willing to do.

What a sobering thought! Am I holding back because I am afraid God will ask me to:

—teach a Sunday school or Bible school class?
—witness to my neighbor?
—give up something that I hold dear?
—lose a loved one?
—move away from my friends and family?
—go to the mission field?

Although God required some rather difficult things of Abraham, he trusted God completely. Because of Abraham's obedience and faith in God, he was called the Friend of God. Does my response to God's requirements show that I too, am His friend?

Faith Builders

READ: Jeremiah 33:3; Luke 17:5;
Hebrews 11:6; I John 5:4

We didn't pray for this—vehicle breakdowns, a hospitalized child, and a big hospital bill.

Or did we?

Then we remembered that we asked God to stretch our faith, to put within us a deeper dependence on Him, and to send experiences to promote trust and growth in Him.

On the field, in a remote jungle station, there were countless instances where our only resource was God Himself. He was all we had. We couldn't call any telephone number for help (there was none). We weren't able to call for a mechanic when our dory motor gave out on a rough sea. We depended on God during the birth of our second child when advanced medical aid was hours away. When village tensions were thick and church stresses were thicker, we believed that God had answers for us. When neighboring villages threatened to tie up my husband and the other believers who accompanied him, we called on God. When I thought my husband was lost at sea (how could I know?—no communication for nearly a day), I poured out my heart to God.

Yes, faith builders, answers to prayer. Plenty of opportunities to lean the harder, trust Him more. *God is faithful* and *God is in control* are two basic lessons we learned. Elementary? Maybe. But basic.

Now—reentry into a culture where help (any kind)

is just a dial away, or a minute away, or a dollar away. Will we need God as much here?

Because we prayed for God to keep our concept of Him strong, He is still sending us faith builders. Is that why we had a vehicle breakdown as soon as we hit the States? (That happens only in Belize!!) Is that why we had a very sick child four weeks later? And a big hospital bill following? (God answered that one by prompting the hospital to write off the bill because we were a low-income missionary family with no insurance! Thank You, Jesus!)

Our girls needed boots and winter garb. Together we asked Jesus to supply them. Our three-year-old would ask, "When is Jesus going to give us some boots?" They KNEW Jesus gave them when we found just what we wanted at the Goodwill store!! What beautiful faith builders for our girls!

It is our conviction that God would have parents use every opportunity to call on His name FIRST, not as a last resort—in sickness or in health, in poverty or affluence, in good times and adverse times.

It is our persuasion that God would have us daddys and mamas use faith builders at every opportunity to teach our children dependence on GOD, instead of on the telephone or the dollar or people.

When our children see God take us at our word and answer our prayers, and when they see our response of WORSHIP to God, will they not learn that it is safe to pray? And that God is to be trusted?

Faith

READ: Hebrews 11:33-38

When the writer of the Book of Hebrews takes us down the Hall of Faith, he shows us first one side and then the other. The obvious victories are shown first. Later we look at the "defeats."

If we look at them side by side, we see that the faithful conquered kingdoms *and* were chained in prison. The faithful administered justice *and* faced jeers and floggings as well. They shut lions' mouths, but were also stoned. On the one hand they quenched flames, and on the other hand they were sawed in two. Some escaped the sword and others were killed with the sword.

How can this be? I thought the strong in faith were only the ones with "direct answers to prayer." Weren't those whose lives ended in death the weak in faith? Yet I see under the names of the latter this inscription: "Of whom the world was not worthy."

Faith looks for a city with sure foundations.

Faith accepts either life or death, suffering or deliverance, with the quiet confidence that God is in control.

Faith knows that with God all is victory.

205

Humility

READ: Luke 14:7-14

When the great Japanese Christian, Kagawa, was living in the slums of Kobe, helping the despised and destitute, he invited a distinguished preacher to speak at a public meeting. Wearing the garments of the poor with whom he lived, Kagawa met his guest at the train. But the guest, mistaking him for a porter, ordered, "Here, fellow, carry my bags. I'm looking for Kagawa."

Kagawa obediently carried the bags of this leader whose outlook upon greatness was so far from the Spirit of Christ that he could not recognize humility when he saw it. *

"For whosoever exalteth himself shall be abased; and he that humbleth himself shall be exalted" (Luke 14:11).

Kagawa forgot himself as he humbly served his fellowman. Today he is remembered as a great man of God. The distinguished preacher who met him that day at the train is forgotten.

> Lord, show me what it means
> To have a humble heart;
> Lord, show me what it means
> To love the world like You;
> Lord, show me what it means
> To love You more each day.

> -Selected

* Copied by permission of Herald Press, from *Spirit Fruit* by John Drescher.

206

The Costly Ornament

READ: I Peter 3:1-6

"Meekness is
that temper of spirit in which we accept [God's] dealings with us as good, and therefore without disputing . . .

"Meekness [is]
first of all a meekness before God, [and] is also such in the face of men, even of evil men, out of a sense that these, with the insults and injuries which they may inflict, are permitted and employed by Him for the chastening and purifying of His elect . . .

"Meekness is
[the] equanimity of spirit that is neither elated nor cast down, simply because it is not occupied with self at all." *

Meekness brings
freedom from anger and bitterness when my loved one is suddenly snatched from me.

Meekness gives
power to forgive when another has betrayed my confidence, using my words to condemn me before others.

Meekness grasps
opportunities for growth in humility and love when I am purposely overlooked and ignored.

207

Meekness faces
kindly those who intentionally make false accusations against me. Yes, even when it is my own sister in the church.

Meekness frees
from irritation over minor things—when my husband is late for dinner or the children spill lime juice.

Meekness believes
that ALL things work together for good when I love God with all my being.

Meekness is
the yoke I take with the truly meek One, my loving Lord JESUS.

* from *An Expository Dictionary of New Testament Words*, by W. E. Vine, published by Fleming H. Revell Company, Old Tappan, NJ.

Contentment

READ: Psalm 34:1-10

"What's your mother doing today?" I asked a little girl who came to our house.

"Nothing," was her simple reply.

Nothing! How can she have nothing to do when I seem to have everything to do? My comparing with others deepened my discontent.

Then one evening our son asked, "What does 'Lord willing' mean?"

"Well, when we plan things, we say 'Lord willing' because the Lord may have something else He wants us to do, and we want to be happy to do whatever He wants," I carefully explained to him.

My thoughts went on . . .

Contentment is sweetness when my plans for the day are upset by crying children, numerous spills, and countless interruptions.

Contentment is a calmness and relaxation in spirit through the day. It is concentrating with gratefulness on the small portions of work completed, and beginning another portion only as I can do so relaxed in spirit. Driving myself and enduring with teeth gritted is neither noble nor patient.

Contentment is refusing to rehearse a mental list of annoyances, but rather, rejoicing in the abundance of my blessings.

Contentment is peace within, knowing I am where God wants me to be, doing what He wants me to do, and knowing I am growing in His likeness.

209

A Prayer for Sweetness

READ: II Corinthians 2:14-17

Lord,
    You are the essence of sweetness.
    Your Son is called the Rose of Sharon.
    Infuse Your sweetness into us.
    We, who are wives and mothers,
    We touch so many other people
    And they touch us.
Sometimes, Lord,
    We get tired of being touched.
    We get upset, irritable.
    Then it takes so little to make us sour.
    And it seems to take so much to make us sweet
    again.
Those little irritations:
    a naughty child,
    a caller buying on credit,
    a thoughtless act,
    someone taking us for granted,
    a breathless, hot day.
So many things come to drain away our sweetness!
Oh, Lord,
    How much we need You then.
    Teach us to crucify the self that feels these slights.
    Teach us to look beyond the slights.

Teach us to hate that sourness that is so displeasing to You and so upsetting to those around us.
And there is no better place to learn than at the feet of Jesus.
Lord,
You know our frame,
A physical frame that feels heat and dirt and sweat and weariness (especially these hot days).
An emotional frame that feels tension and the effects of Daddy being gone.
A spiritual frame that bows under burdens of unsaved souls and problems within the church.
Is it perhaps unrealistic to expect ourselves to stay sweet in the face of our limitations?
Oh, but Lord,
You said, "My grace is sufficient for thee."
You said too that Christ by the Spirit abides in us and He brings with Him the fullness of Your riches for our needs.
So, Lord,
We come once more to ask Your aid.
Keep us sweet. Give us pleasant words to say (especially to our husbands at the end of the day).
Help us to keep a merry heart and a cheerful face.
In our weakness we lean on You, believing Your power can keep us sweet.

For Jesus' sake,
Amen.

211

Inward Beauty

READ: I Samuel 16:6-13

Sighing, I view my reflection in the mirror. If only I could shed those excess pounds and do something to control my wayward hair. If only I were beautiful. . . .

The image of a dear friend comes to mind. She is one whom the kindest would call plain.

In spite of this, I am convinced that my friend is beautiful. She is one of the kindest persons I know. One particular way she has is that she is a gifted letter writer and has a knack for sending me uplifting letters just when I need them most. Always included is a lovely thinking-of-you card with just the right message for the time.

Once I asked her how she knew when to send her cards and letters to encourage me at times when I was so blue. She denied ever knowing in advance of my needs. I cannot believe this is a mere coincidence. I feel that she is in tune with God.

Turning from the mirror, I no longer am wishing for outward beauty, but inward beauty. After all, that is what counts!

Diamond in Refinement

READ: Ephesians 1

It was Saturday morning.
  I unloaded again—to my husband.
  It happens quite frequently these days.
He listens.
  He reassures. . . .
  It's just what I want.
I cried—
  felt so weak,
  sorta like a failure,
  caught up in the super-missionary,
    perfect-parent syndrome.
  When I make a mistake,
    I feel like a zero.
I told him, "I belong on the rubbish heap."
He said, "You're in the diamond box, Honey."
Oh. Really, God?
That valuable?
  . . . a diamond in the rough, though. . . .
I see, God, You're using people and circumstances
  and hurts and misunderstandings
to chip away the rough edges,
  to refine and polish.
So often I delay the refining process
  by resisting the tools You're using.
But everything You send to me
  is meant for good.

So I cast myself on You,
  the Master Jeweler.
You know what You're doing,
  who I am,
  what I am becoming—
  that's good to know.

213

Growth

READ: II Peter 1:1-8

Let me be a little kinder;
Let me be a little blinder
  To the faults of those about me;
  Let me praise a little more;
Let me be, when I am weary,
Just a little bit more cheery;
  Let me serve a little better
  Those that I am striving for.

Let me be a little braver
When temptations bid me waver;
  Let me strive a little harder
  To be all that I should be;
Let me be a little meeker
With the brother that is weaker;
  Let me think more of my neighbor
  And a little less of me.

Let me be a little sweeter;
Make my life a bit completer,
  By doing what I should do
  Every minute of the day.
Let me toil without complaining,
Not a humble task disdaining,
  Let me face the summons calmly
  When death beckons me away.

—Author Unknown

Accept the Situation and Praise God

READ: Romans 8:26-31

"Those hard situations are put into your lives to change you. Stop praying for them to change, but pray that they may change you." —H. Markham

The Lord has been cleansing me of deep unwillingness to accept all He allows and teaching me to thank Him, seeing He is allowing it all to consume my dross and to refine my gold.

If I find I cannot accept any situation and thank Him for it, then I come to Him confessing, "Lord, I am not willing to thank You for this, but I choose to accept all with thanks."

Then I begin to say as those difficult situations arise, or depression comes upon me, or I lose my peace over my own wrongdoing or the wrongdoing of others, or I become frustrated with accidents or ill health, "My Father, this is another one of those things You are allowing to consume my dross and to refine my gold, and I thank You for it."

As I continue to accept the situation and give thanks, I soon see He is changing me. And now I would not have had the situation changed as I see what He has been doing in me through it and as I learn to accept all with thanksgiving.

—Erma Maust: Used by permission.

215

Uninvited Christmas Guest

READ: I Thessalonians 5:16-24

I squeezed my eyes shut tightly, trying to keep back the tears. As my husband asked God to bless our Christmas dinner, I chafed inwardly.

Why did Gustavo have to come just before dinner? Why had my husband invited him to stay? Didn't we have the right to eat a meal alone, especially on Christmas Day?

I knew I should give "hospitality without grudging." But I begrudged Gustavo a share of the Christmas meal I had so lovingly prepared for our family. I didn't want to feel this way. I felt angry, guilty, and frustrated.

"Forgive me, Lord," I begged. "Please teach me. How can I give hospitality without grudging on this occasion?"

In a flash, I thought of the words, "In everything give thanks."

"Maybe that's the way, Lord. I don't feel very thankful, but I'll try. Thank You that we have plenty of food to share. There's more than enough for us. Thank You for my husband and children. Gustavo doesn't have a happy family. I guess I can share mine with him. (But did it have to be today?) Thank You for giving me more practice in giving hospitality without

216

grudging. I need it. Thank You that Gustavo came for Christmas dinner."

It wasn't easy. I still wasn't overjoyed about having an uninvited Christmas guest. But giving thanks helped me to accept the situation.

It has also helped me many times since then. God keeps giving me opportunities to practice the skill of giving hospitality without grudging.

In everything give thanks. It works.

217

It Matters Not

READ: Hebrews 12:1-15

It matters not if I've been hurt;
   It matters not at all
That sometimes from my weary eyes
   The scalding teardrops fall.
What matters most is if I've erred
   And not confessed the sin,
And through my lack some needy soul
   Has failed to follow Him.

It matters not if cherished friends
   On whom I've leaned in vain
Have wounded me by word and deed
   And left me with my pain.
What matters is—can I forgive
   Again and yet again?
'Tis not "Have they been true?" but "Lord,
   Have I been true to them?"

'Twill matter not when evening comes
   How rough the road I've trod,
If only I have walked with Him
   And led some soul to God!
For when I wake to be like Him
   Who saved me by His grace,
Earth's pain will vanish when I catch
   One glimpse of His dear face!

      —Alice Hansche Mortenson:
      Used by permission

A Child Forgives

READ: Matthew 6:9-15

One of the advantages of being a missionary is the privilege of homeschooling. I enjoy being with my children and seeing them learn. I'm glad I can teach my own.

Sometimes, however, the job seems overwhelming. Interruptions frustrate me. Trying to prepare dinner and teach at the same time, I sometimes get uptight and rushed. Time pressure mounts as mealtime approaches.

One particularly hectic morning, Timmy seemed to resist my efforts to help him learn. I lost control and yelled at him. Immediately remorseful, I apologized and he forgave me.

Awhile later I looked over Timmy's shoulder to see how he was doing. What I saw nearly made me cry. To write a sentence using the word "love," Timmy had written, "My mother is love."

How could he write that when I had acted so unlovingly? Then I knew. Timmy had forgiven and forgotten.

Jesus said we should become as little children. How often we hold grudges. We lick the wounds of past hurts long after the offenses should be forgotten. May God help us to be childlike and forgiving.

"Brethren, be not children in understanding: howbeit in malice be ye children, but in understanding be men" (I Corinthians 14:20).

219

Instant Obedience

READ: Exodus 19:1-8; 32:1-6

We were reminded at our church's annual Women's Workshop that our children need to be taught to obey instantly. I knew this was something needed in our home and made a mental note of the idea.

I shared the events of the day at the supper table that evening. The subject of instant obedience was discussed and the need in our home acknowledged.

Minutes later as I cleared away the supper dishes, my husband noticed me snacking on the leftovers. Realizing my inability to help myself, he asked me to stop.

My response was one of resistance, nothing "instant" about it! I was smitten as I remembered our supper conversation and decided that Mother had better learn a few lessons first!

"Teach me thy way, O Lord!"

CHAPTER NINE

"I Will Incline Mine Ear to a Parable"

Psalm 49:4

Vessels—Useless or Useful

READ: Romans 9:14-24

Several years ago I needed a new water pitcher. One day I stopped at a garage sale on my way to town. Imagine my delight as I spied a beautiful glass pitcher for only 25 cents. Its tall, stately form seemed to say, "I'm just what you are looking for."

Soon the day came when I had company and I could use my new pitcher. As I poured the water shortly before the meal, I discovered why the pitcher was marked only 25 cents. The spout was designed in such a way that when you poured, the water would run down the side of the vessel, spilling all over the table. It was of no use to me.

Later as I thought about it, I wondered how many times I am like that pitcher. Perhaps I look like I could be useful to the Master but yet I have too much of ME in the way. When God tries to use me, the work is hampered by an unyielding, selfish pride. Unless Christ is allowed to have His way in me, my vessel too, is useless. I must give myself to the Potter to fashion as He sees best. He removes the impurities and starts to reshape me. Self is no longer alive to defend its position. In God's own loving way, He applies most of the pressure on the inside just as a potter does in shaping a vessel, urging me to expand

222

for greater usefulness.

When He is satisfied I can be useful, the Potter gently places me in the fire. He knows exactly how long it will take and at what temperature to make me a vessel that can stand the test. It is a gradual process that will fit me for each task as it comes.

It is my desire that the next time I am placed in the fire, I will remember I am a vessel of mercy and can learn to know the riches of His glory.

Motives Make the Difference

READ: Luke 7:36-50

While Jesus was eating with a Pharisee one day, a very sinful woman came to Him weeping. She washed His feet with her tears and dried them with her hair. She also anointed them with a costly ointment and kissed them.

The Pharisee was convinced that Jesus was not a prophet or He would have known what kind of a woman she was. But the woman had had a glimpse of the holiness of God's Son, which produced in her an attitude of reverence and fear as compared with her own undoneness.

Later, as Jesus journeyed toward the cross, He received another kiss. It was the kiss of betrayal into the hands of wicked men. Judas seemed to see only the thirty pieces of silver. He could not see the greedy heart which stole his love for the Master he had followed for three years.

It was not the action in these two examples that made the difference in the eternal destiny of the woman and Judas, for it was much the same. But it was their motives.

Motives are something we can't see. Many times I am guilty of looking at another person's action and mistaking it for their motive. I am the only person who can evaluate my motives in the truest sense.

A few examples could be: Do I really need the items I buy or do I buy simply because someone else does.

Do I attend sewing circle, go to rest home services, and visit school out of duty, or do I have a lively interest in the work of the church and school?

As I invite guests, do I hope they will notice my dishes, food, a new piece of furniture, and my accomplishments? Or do I have a longing for the fellowship we can share as we visit?

May I catch a glimpse of Jesus as this woman did. It is only in looking to Jesus that our motives can glorify God.

A Childlike Heart

READ: Psalm 91

'Tween the crashing,
'Twixt the flashing,
In a storm, one summer eve,
My little girl
Came to my side,
Said, "Mama, are you scared?
I wish Daddy
Would be home.
Mama, I'm afraid—let's pray."
So we knelt
To ask protection
Through the storm. So dark the day.
As we arose
She had forgotten
She had been afraid at all.
Going on, she
Played as usual,
Knowing soon the storm would lull.
I thought, "My child,
How different
From when I in God confide!"
The angry surges
Of self-pity,
Hatred, envy, hurt, and pride,

Sweep o'er my soul.
I battle and pour
My heart to God above.
Then I arise
Thinking He'll
Need help to bear the burden because—
It's quite a load
For one to bear.
I'll carry a portion and a part.
Oh, for the faith
Of a little child!
Lord, give me a childlike heart.

The Christian's Sure Retreat

READ: Psalm 61

The fresh, fluffy snow which had lain so peacefully in a soft blanket was being driven into impassable drifts by the fierce north wind. Bone-chilling temperatures made the small remodeled garage, which was our temporary meeting place, seem like a haven as we gathered to worship.

Not only had it been a shelter from the northern winters and summer rains, but it had been a shelter for our souls as unitedly we sought God.

As we gathered on this stormy February day, my mind was drawn to the many shelters God has provided for those who serve Him.

There is the shelter in brotherhood. A kindred spirit is shared, and love is felt so keenly. It is a place where we can rejoice and weep together with those we have learned to love.

The shelter of a Christian home is a blessing we so often take for granted. May our home be guided in a way that it can truly be a shelter from the demanding cares of the world. Each one who dwells there needs the shelter of being understood in a relaxed atmosphere.

We have the shelter of our secret closet as we fall on our knees before God and lay our burden at His feet, the shelter of knowing He can carry us through those times of storm and turbulence when we cannot possibly see ahead.

We can have the shelter of a clear conscience as we give our wills completely to Him.

May we have complete confidence in the shelter of the Saviour's love, that our children can see there is no other refuge in these troubled times.

We are also promised an eternal shelter with Him when the storms of life are over. May this be our goal as we continue to hide our souls in Him.

Caught by Surprise!

READ: Matthew 25:1-13

It happened again! We came home from church and found the telltale evidence of sand on the floor inside the basement window. Someone had been in the house. For several weeks this was going on. We knew someone must be aware of the times we were all away from the house. Not much was missing, just a few small items. But it was upsetting and could lead to something more serious. Who could it be?

The following Sunday our youth worker decided to slip home from church an hour early. And sure enough, a fifteen-year-old neighbor boy was wandering about in the house. Imagine his surprise and terror! He begged Marvin not to call the police or tell my husband. He said this was the *first* time he had ever done it. He promised to come to church every Sunday!

This incident reminded me of Christ's second coming. Many people will be caught by complete surprise. They may not be doing anything really bad, just living a life of disobedience to the divine laws of God and thinking they are getting by with it. Their cries for mercy and lying excuses and promises to do better will not help at that time. Our young friend had another chance to change his ways. But when Christ returns, there will be no more mercy for those who are "caught by surprise."

How Much Do I Care?

READ: Psalm 142:1-4

It was a windy, sub-zero morning. I watched Vernon leave for his 20-mile trip over frozen lakes and portages to another Indian village. The trails would be hard to see with the new snow, but he had traveled the way before, and we felt confident he would make it through all right. Three hours later we had a phone call from the village saying Vernon hadn't arrived. In spite of the strong wind, several men went to look for him and traveled the 20-mile route without seeing any sign of him. Then we realized how serious the situation really was! Aircraft were alerted to fly over the area and many snowmobiles went out, exploring all the possible trails Vernon could have mistaken for the right one. One by one they returned from their unsuccessful search. Many phone calls were made to alert friends and family. Prayer groups gathered to pray for his safety. More than ten hours had passed since he had left our house. I felt he couldn't possibly be alive anymore in this bitterly cold weather.

And then the phone rang and we heard the unbelievable news that Vernon was found . . . and alive! He had gone many miles on a wrong trail and then got stuck. So he walked to the nearest shore, built a fire, and waited for help. With rejoicing, we shared the good news with everyone.

This incident had a happy ending. But what about those countless people who are still out there, going on the wrong trails of life, deeply stuck in the clutches of Satan, and no one is looking for them? No one is risking his life to find them and bring them into the warm fold of the Shepherd. What am I willing to sacrifice for people's *eternal* safety? Do I really care? Do you?

The Product Is Good . . .
Will I Pay the Price?

READ: I John 1

The young salesman did an excellent job demonstrating his vacuum sweeper to me. He was sure it would take care of all my cleaning needs and many other household chores. It would deep clean much below the surface dirt which is so destructive to my furnishings. I would save a lot of money in not having to replace furniture and carpeting or buy other tools. It was a marvelous machine indeed! And all for just a few dollars a day. I was attracted to it and saw it was able to do all he claimed it could. But I had to decide whether it was in my budget and whether it was a priority to me to invest that much in a vacuum sweeper.

After he left, I mused on the many parallels of this incident to evangelism. As the salesman, I need to be persuaded about the Product, the Gospel of Jesus Christ. As I present it, I must demonstrate by my life that it really works. I saw that what my salesman claimed his vacuum sweeper could do, the Gospel can do in a spiritual sense. It can touch every area of people's lives. It can "deep clean" and not just take care of surface problems. The deposit to be paid each day, I saw to be the daily commitment it takes to live in victory after one receives the Lord Jesus into his life. But everyone has to decide personally whether he will "purchase." Is it my highest priority? Do I really want it? And am I willing to pay the daily price of commitment to be a victorious and fruitful Christian?

233

The Fire of God

READ: I Corinthians 3:11-15

In my dream I saw my grandfather's old barn on fire. Desperately I tried to call the fire department but couldn't reach them. Then I saw my husband come on the scene. I expected him to rush in and try to save the contents. Instead, he calmly said, "There really isn't anything in the barn worth saving." Then I awoke.

Dreams. Do they have meaning? Does God ever teach us things through a dream? There are many accounts in the Bible where God spoke to people through dreams. Jacob, Joseph, Solomon, Daniel, and Pilate's wife are just a few examples. Certainly if we want to attach significance to our dreams today, the interpretation needs to correspond with the Word of God. And the dream will no doubt be something you have been thinking about and something the Lord is wanting to teach you.

The day before I had this dream about the burning barn, we were in a gathering with fellow missionaries. The visiting speaker was an experienced missionary and had spiritual depth that challenged all of us. He spoke about being on fire for the Lord and gave an illustration to show how everyone is attracted to a burning building. So maybe that's why I had this

234

dream!

As I thought of the possible meaning and purpose of my dream, I observed that fire also destroys useless material. Perhaps God saw things in my life that aren't worth keeping. What about those pet sins of envy, self-pity, worry, and inner hostility that lurk in the corners of my life? I really don't want to salvage any of those things when the Fire of God starts burning in my life. "Burn on, O Fire of God, and purify me for Yourself and Your work."

235

Fit Only for Garbage

READ: Revelation 3:14-19

The four perfectly shaped loaves were ready for the oven. My family would be pleased to have freshly baked bread for supper. I turned on the oven, put the bread in, and watched it slowly rise to full size. The unmistakable aroma filled the kitchen. But halfway through the baking time, something happened. The heating element burned out! What could I do with this half-baked bread? Desperately I tried to think of something: toast? dressing? dog food? As the bread cooled and shrank to an ugly lump, I realized it wasn't fit for any of these, but only to throw to the garbage.

The Lord taught me a lesson through this. Sometimes I'm like this half-baked bread. I fail to stay in the heat and warmth of God's love and His Word. At first everything seems to be normal. But as I cool off, I shrink spiritually, and become ineffective with people and out of fellowship with the Lord. I may even blame other people for my condition. Sometimes I frantically try to salvage or cover up my lukewarmness by increased activity. But God wants me to stop, admit my failure, receive forgiveness, and start over, just like I had to do with my bread. Then I can again experience His love and burning in my heart and be a vessel fit for the master's use.

The Sprain

READ: Psalm 133

Keith sprained his wrist. Severe pain distracted him from other planned activities. Oh, for an elastic bandage to totally immobilize the tormented member. Ice water helped a little.

Next day Chico suggested a treatment from his grandmother Onelia.

"She fixes sprains."

A few hours later Keith stopped at her little house.

"It feels better now," he reported on his arrival at home.

Three days later he returned for a checkup. I was present too.

Onelia explained how in a sprain the bones at the back of the wrist are sprung apart.

"Not close, not close," she emphasized.

Smoothing on ointment, she stroked the arm firmly from the elbow down. Repeatedly she massaged toward the wrist. Next she grasped the forearm below the elbow and closed her hand strongly. Very, very slowly she moved toward the hand pressing the bones together.

"When I squeezed the wrist," Onelia recalled, "he moved and gasped."

"Because it hurt," I commented.

237

"Of course, it hurts," she answered. "Last week a man working in my front yard sprained his ankle. I worked on it, but he cried, 'Stop! It hurts!' So I stopped. It didn't get better. Days later he came back, but by then it was swollen and I couldn't feel the bones. I couldn't do anything to help."

How like human relationships this is! People who once were close are sprung apart. The pain is constant.

God's remedy is to acknowledge mistakes, admit outright all misdeeds and openly repent of vindictive actions and comments.

But pride will be hurt. Why should we confess and perhaps uncover our own drastic failings? How can we acknowledge that we don't want to be reconciled and set up a happy relationship? Very soon swelling obscures the basic issues. Pain has gone on so long we decide to let it fade by itself. Often a working relationship is never regained.

—Rosa Mae Mullet. Used by permission.

238

Who Are You Fooling?

READ: Genesis 38:1-26

It was a motherly check. A check on what my children were doing during closing prayer.

I caught her. One eye was twitching with the effort to keep it tightly closed. The other eye was peeking at the chick her feet were trying to chase. Who did she think she was fooling?

Suddenly, God showed me how I was just like my four-year-old daughter. Who did I think I was fooling? One eye was shut—the eye other people could see. The other one was wide open, toying with my supper menu, formulating a plan to correct LouAnn, and wondering how long *this* Kekchi prayer would last.

God nudged me. I shut my eye and prayed, "Oh, God, forgive me." Then I began interceding for each person around the room. The prayer was not long enough. The *jocan taxak* (amen) was said before I had reached the third person.

Touch of Toothpaste
or Mess of Milk

READ: Matthew 7:1-5

"Mommy, you should see what Jonathan did!" Big sister came running to tell on her little brother. "He squeezed toothpaste on the couch."

As she came bounding down the steps, her dress caught on the milk pail sitting at the top of the steps. The full pail dumped. Milk splashed onto the freezer below, ran in rivulets down the steps, and soaked into her dress and mine. My immediate reaction was one of annoyance. Later I told her that she should take a lesson from this, meaning of course, that she should stop tattling.

Then I started thinking. Did God intend the lesson for me also? How many times have I run to Him over a little dab of toothpaste in my sister's life and on the way I've made a mess of milk? A mess that took ten times as much time and trouble to clean up.

Like the times her fault is an unkind glance and mine is a volley of words. Or hers is an unthoughtful oversight and I responded with grouchiness that lasted all day.

And why do I behold the dab of toothpaste in my sister's life and consider not the spilled milk in my own?

"It is only imperfection that is intolerant of the imperfect. The more perfect we are, the more gentle we become toward the defects of others." *

Pineapple Eyes

READ: John 6:48-58

Marsha was only seven months old, but she talked to me one day. I sat down in the rocking chair to nurse her and she couldn't suck, though she was hungry. Puzzled, I looked in her mouth. Yes, there was the problem. She had a pineapple eye in there and the juice, what juice there had been, was completely sucked out. She made no objection to my removing it. She seemed relieved to be rid of it.

How often do I come to the Lord with a sucked-out pineapple eye in my mouth, hindering me from getting the true nourishment of the Word?

Did I say Marsha talked to me? Out of the mouth of a babe I was instructed to let the Lord remove the pineapple eyes as gently and lovingly as I did hers, offering no resistance.

"Open thy mouth wide, and I will fill it" (Psalm 81:10).

And God Calls Us Sheep!

READ: Ezekiel 34:11-16

I have no experience with sheep, but one day I observed their obstinancy firsthand. A big old ram thought the grass was greener on the other side of the fence and got his head stuck in the process. In sympathy, my sister-in-law and I struggled to free him. Our feeble pushes were no match for his determined pushes against us. We started to walk away in disgust, but he looked too pathetic. He lay there so stupidly, as if he would die before he thought of a way of escape; so dumb—not even a bleat for help.

A new strategy struck us: if pushing his head backwards made him strain forward, reverse psychology might work. With fists clenching his wooly head, we tugged instead of pushing. The sheep jerked his head, and with a mighty heave backwards, loosed himself from his trap. Free! And so easy! He had been too ignorant to free himself and too ornery to let us free him, until we made him more uncomfortable in his plight.

And God calls us sheep! Has He ever pulled my hair? Now I know it was out of pity. What traps does my selfishness get me into? How helpless I am to free myself! How ignorant of His kind ways to release me. But oh, how glad I am that He is so fond of me, His foolish sheep.

Healing

READ: Exodus 15:23-27

Their twenty-foot-wide Kekchi skirts swirl commandingly as two Indian mothers swish into my house.

"We want medicine for our babies' sores," the more aggressive one demands. I examine the first baby.

"Has the doctor seen your baby?"

"Yes."

"Did he give you a prescription?"

"Yes."

"Did you buy the medicine?"

"No."

"Why not?"

"I lost the paper."

"Well, my advice is to ask the doctor for another paper and buy what it says."

"The medicine you gave me the other day didn't help at all," the second mother accuses.

Surely, I hadn't missed my diagnosis of obvious scabies. "Are you sure you applied the cream I gave you?"

Rather sheepishly she admits the truth.

"No." I watch two Kekchi mothers turn away without medicine.

Healing! My own aching heart desperately needs it. Did I lose God's prescription? Or am I refusing to apply the balm He offers? Or do I hear His comforting words, "Keep on. You are taking the right medicine. It just takes time to do its work."

Future Hindsight

READ: II Corinthians 4:16—5:1

Sometimes when I read a storybook that gets too boring or tense or sad, I flip to the last pages to see how it ends so I have the courage to wade through the middle of the story.

In today's page of the storybook of my life, I long to do the same, to run ahead so I can look back at today and find meaning in this jumble.

God actually provided for that longing! I *do* know how this light affliction of today and tomorrow is going to end! With that heavenly anticipation, let me wade through the middle of the story today.

Buggy Beans

READ: James 3:1-12

When we came to El Salvador, I was an inexperienced bride. I didn't even know how to cook beans. My husband liked Pennsylvania Dutch cooking better anyway, and, eager to please him, I served potatoes and gravy.

Trouble was, I had to cook for a large number of other mission workers besides my husband. So once in a while, out of a sense of duty, I'd try to cook beans. Sometimes they burned. Often they were too dry or too hard. They didn't taste good. In order to protect my reputation as a cook, I avoided cooking beans.

So it was that one day when I opened the bean canister, I found it crawling with bugs.

Clapping the lid back on, I wondered what to do. What would the other workers think of me? The beans were mission property. I had let them spoil. Did that mean I was a bad missionary?

I didn't want anyone to know it.

I tiptoed to the door, looked both ways, then tossed out the buggy beans. In the lush grass, they didn't show at all.

Days later, a row of sturdy bean plants stood boldly in the lawn. Unfortunately, I wasn't the first to notice.

"Look at this row of beans," I overheard one worker

say to another. "Why would anyone have planted beans in the yard?"

"They're planted awfully thick. Why, it looks like someone just pitched a bunch of beans out the door. Now, who would've done something like that?"

I hoped they'd never know.

I did eventually learn to cook beans. The natives taught me to add onions, garlic, salt, and plenty of water. Now we like them.

I've also learned that careless words are like the beans I tossed out that day. Sometimes I think the unkind things I say about others won't be repeated. Too often they are. Ugly situations crop up just like those beans did when I threw them out the door.

Lord, help me be careful about the words that fall from my lips. Let me not toss them out thoughtlessly. "Set a watch, O Lord, before my mouth; keep the door of my lips" (Psalm 141:3).

Turned Away

READ: Revelation 21:22-27

The memory of the disappointed young man at the airport haunts me. He was with a group of peasants leaving for Houston. Probably because of overbooking, he was turned back from the gate of departure.

As the impact of the words "NO ROOM" hit him, he stared in hurt, anger, and disappointment. He dropped his brand-new travel bag with a thud. I think if he would have been just a little younger he would have cried.

It got me thinking about those who will be turned away from heaven's door, not because of overbooking or lack of space, but because of sin. The disappointed young man was probably able to find a later flight. But those who are turned away from heaven will have no more opportunity.

Lord, cleanse me from sin and anything that would keep me out of heaven. Let me help others get in, too.

Culvert in Flood Time

READ: Ephesians 6:13-18

From our kitchen window, I have a good view of the dome-shaped culvert through which the small stream bubbles peacefully. But with the heavy rains of rainy season, the pressure builds up as muddy, rushing waters funnel to the culvert which is inadequate for flood time.

To me, that culvert in flood time is a picture of being pressured. On sunny days when things bubble smoothly on, I can be pleasant and cheerful and kind. But under pressure—and how much it seems I face it—I find it easy to be angry, unkind, impatient, and cross if I'm not prepared.

"Prepared" is being ready ahead of the need. (Flood time is not the time to prepare.) I need to find my strength in God, delighting in Him, meditating on His Word, and realizing His presence at the beginning of the day and throughout the day however pressing the work appears or how full the day promises to be. Then when things come thick and fast and the pressure begins to build up, I am calm within and handling the pressures as they come. I am adequate in the flood time because my Lord "enlarges me in distress" as I am prepared and looking to Him.

Chocolate Chips and Sins

READ: I Corinthians 10:1-13

When I was 16, I went to help some friends with a new baby. While there I was asked to make some cookies.

The recipe was an oatmeal one that called for goodies such as coconut, raisins, nuts, and chocolate chips. As I was mixing the dough, their oldest girl informed me not to sample the chocolate chips.

"For some odd reason," she explained, "they have a bitter taste and leave an aftertaste in your mouth that's hard to get rid of, but they're all right once baked."

Of course, I should have heeded her advice. I did believe her, but her warning made me curious, so I sampled them anyway.

I regretted it. Just as she had said, I had this horrible aftertaste that took awhile to leave although the very first taste (when I popped a chip into my mouth) was good and sweet just like chocolate chips are supposed to be!

How like sin. Often Satan tempts us with things that we have been warned about by others who have already "tasted" and found that it causes a bitter aftertaste. How many of us have to taste it anyway just to make sure?

My prayer: Dear Lord, help me to learn from the mistakes and/or advice of others so that my own life will be free of "bitter aftertastes" that I could have avoided if only I had heeded!

Gentle Wisdom

READ: James 3:13-18

My doctor, while I was in the States undergoing tests, was a very intelligent neurologist. He knew exactly what tests he wanted done and in what order. His early morning visits were brief and to the point: this is what he wanted done today.

While my doctor "had it all" medically speaking, we found out he lacked other desirable characteristics. He had little sympathy or patience with balking patients! One of the tests scheduled was a bit risky and the law required those in charge to tell us about the risks involved. My husband was understandably reluctant to have me take the test. He tried to ask my neurologist a little about it and whether it was really necessary. The doctor, however, was rather brusque with my husband's anxiety and made him feel quite stupid. Later another doctor took time to explain more about the test and soothe my husband's feelings.

After we returned to Belize, a little girl came to my door one day. I don't remember what she wanted, but I know I answered her a bit brusquely. After she left, I started thinking about my neurologist.

I suppose my knowledge of the world and how things work was, in many ways, as far above the little girl's as my doctor's knowledge was above mine. One of the secrets of true wisdom, however, is to be able to handle knowledge on the level of those with whom we work. Knowledge framed in loving words and humble, gentle deeds is much more easily understood and certainly more appreciated.

"And as ye would that men should do to you, do ye also to them likewise" (Luke 6:31).

You Are Unique!

READ: I Corinthians 12:12-27

An ancient legend tells of a king who walked into his gardens one day and found almost everything withered and dying. The oak tree was sick of life because it was not tall and beautiful like the pine. The pine was upset, for it could not bear fruit like the pear tree, while the pear tree complained that it did not have the lovely odor of the spruce. The same discontent prevailed throughout the garden. But when the king came to the pansy, he saw its bright face full of cheerfulness.

"Well, little flower," said the monarch, "I'm glad to find at least one tiny plant that is happy."

"Your Majesty," said the pansy, "I know I am small, but I decided you wanted a pansy when you planted me here. If you had desired an oak or a pear tree, you would have put one in my place. So I've determined to be the best little pansy I can be!"

As parts of Christ's body, we have a special place in His plan. He has given us unique gifts and abilities with which to serve Him. The Apostle Paul uses a description of our physical bodies to help us understand the relationship of one to another in the church, the body of Christ. We should not try to function as the "eye" when we are called to serve as the "foot."

Instead of copying the talents of others, we need to use the abilities that God has given us to His honor and glory.

In order for the church to function properly we need to exercise our gifts willingly. If we have the gift of teaching, we should teach whenever God asks us to, even if it is more often than someone else. Perhaps you are asked to do some mundane task—do it willingly. Like the cheerful little pansy, bloom where you are planted!

Danger—Just Ahead
READ: Judges 16:4-21

The little blue car I had hit spun in circles on the ice and finally came to a rest. Thankfully no one was hurt beyond a few bumps and scratches.

After I had left the scene of the accident, I wondered what God was trying to teach me. As I had driven up the icy hill, suddenly there was a car right in front of me. The other driver had seen the car behind me in the distance but had failed to see the immediate danger right before her eyes.

Many times we can see spiritual danger far off better than the danger that is lurking just over the next hill or around the next curve.

We think about what that root of bitterness will be like when it grows into hatred while we go on comfortably nursing a grudge.

In the secret of our hearts we may earnestly covet another person's position or gift, unaware of the resulting envy and strife.

We may innocently feed our child's ego, yet detest the very idea of a proud adult.

Lord, open my eyes that I may see the immediate dangers, the little things which I often overlook. I know they will grow into enormous weeds whose roots become embedded in the heart, making them very difficult to remove. Please, Lord, show me immediate dangers and give me the strength and wisdom to avoid them.

CHAPTER TEN

"He Hath Smitten, and He Will Bind Us Up"

Hosea 6:1

Waking Up At Home

READ: I Corinthians 15:51-57

"Baby dear." His daddy took those tiny frail hands into his own big strong ones. "Today is the first day of a new life for you, either on earth with a fixed-up heart, or else a new life in heaven."

Jonathan's one-month-old face returned a weary, puzzled look of pain.

And then he was whisked away to heart surgery
                                        and
                                             to heaven.

Think of stepping on shore
    and finding it heaven,
Of taking hold of a hand
    and finding it God's hand,
Of breathing a new air
    and finding it celestial air,
Of feeling invigorated
    and finding it immortality,
Of passing from storm and tempest
    to an unknown calm,
Of waking up
    and finding it
            HOME.

—Author Unknown

256

Grief

READ: Revelation 21:1-7

The private room was deathly still. The doorknob clicked. In walked the cardiovascular surgeon. He slumped into a chair and wiped the sweat from the defeat lines on his face.

"I'm sorry." He hung his head. "I tried everything I knew. . . ."

We were sorry, too, but there were no words to say, so we didn't say them. My husband started weeping softly.

There were phone calls to make, to grandparents who would never see their tiny grandson alive. On the phone, you have to find some words.

Of the thousands of words I phrased in my mind, only one sentence was worthy to be uttered: "May I hold my baby?"

As I cradled him and stroked his silky hair (his face was too cold), I hoped he looked down from heaven and understood. It was my way of telling him how I had longed to be with him when he died.

I read and reread a line in an imaginary book. "She woodenly gathered up fragments of shattered hopes: handmade booties, a sleeper, a pacifier." Wooden. Numb. Down the hall, past the intensive care waiting room full of dozing parents. They were still hoping. I wanted to announce loudly, "Our baby died. Hope yours makes it." But I didn't. I wasn't in their shoes anymore. For us the anxiety was over. Forever.

Grieving had begun. A new experience. So this is how it felt.

God knew grief too. His only Son died too. But for Him it was different. He could see death from heaven's comfortable mansions. We see death from earth, and it hurts. Hurts terribly.

But Jesus saw death from earth's side. He knew pain. By that, I am healed. By that, heaven is opened to me. I can meet sorrow and suffering surrounded by heaven's comfort.

Thank You, God, for Jesus.

Unwanted Fame

READ: Job 19:23-27

The compiler of this book specifically prayed, "Bring into my sister's life the experiences You want her to share with the rest of us."

Is that why my precious and only baby died? So I could write it in a book and have it published across the nation? I'd have preferred keeping my baby and dropping the "fame." Millions of mothers suffer the same grief and no one notices. Not even their nation's statisticians.

If growing is this painful, I'd prefer not growing. If becoming more useful is so costly, let me remain unuseful.

But no. God is God. I am at peace when I trust His purposes. I don't see growth or usefulness—certainly not in proportion to the pain. But I see God—through a glass, darkly; but then, face to face.

Quieted As a Weaned Child

READ: Psalm 131

A nursing child takes his mother for granted. He demands his milk. A weaning child is fretful and fussy, even angry that his greatest pleasure has been taken from him. A weaned child, however, learns to enjoy his mother as a person, and not merely as a giver of milk. He learns to eat strong meat.

God took away from me the one I loved above all others (besides my husband). My soul was anything but quieted! But even while I was in the fretful, fussy weaning stage, I sensed God's patient father love at work. And now after this, my soul, hope in the Lord—only Him and not His gifts—from henceforth and forever.

Sorrow—Joy *

READ: Mark 16:1-7

Easter.
Easter Monday.
  Will it always bring its sorrow?
  Its bittersweet memories?
Easter.
  I should be joyful.
  Why must the tears come?
I sing,
  "Bring treasures . . .
  thy choicest and thy best
  Before His pierced feet."
I brought my treasure a year ago
But I must bring again
  and again
the desire
  to have those stout little arms around me,
  to see those sparkly eyes,
  to hear him say, "Mommy,"
  to share some little joy
    like first watermelon,
    or fried chicken,
    or a freshly picked flower,
    or a baby bird.
Easter.
I sing,
  "Because He lives, all fear is gone."
He lives!
  I not only have sorrow,
  I have joy.
My treasure is with Jesus!

* Our six-year-old son was killed in a tractor accident on Easter Monday. This was written a year later.

Hope for the Hurting

READ: Psalm 42:6-11

Think of the greatest sorrow, the worst tragedy, or the deepest hurt you ever experienced. God seemed far away, and you felt even your close friends didn't understand. How do you handle calamities?

Sorrow and grief are deep wounds. And wounds hurt. Just about the time you think they are starting to heal, some memory is triggered or you are talking with someone about it, and the tears start flowing again. Deep wounds will hurt for a very long time.

God and time have a marvelous way of healing the hurts that come into our lives. And they *will* heal if the wound doesn't become infected with bitterness, anger, or blame. Occasionally we need to examine ourselves to see if any negative feelings are hindering the healing process. If they are, we can let the tears of repentance flow, and the blood of Jesus will cleanse us. Then the healing can continue.

Recently our family went through a very difficult time which affected all of us very deeply. We felt crushed and wondered if we could ever be happy or smile again. But we knew God was in control and cared about us. Over and over He revealed Himself in unexpected ways. We banded together as a family and in faith claimed the promise that something good

262

would come from the deep hurt.

Have you had a crushing experience, a death of a dream? Maybe it was a family problem, sickness, spiritual defeat, or even a death. God wants to bring healing. Allow Him to keep your wound clean with His love and healing touch. In His time it will heal, and in the meantime you can rejoice in the Lord, even if you do not fully understand the meaning of it all.

Bad News

READ: II Corinthians 1:3-7

Solomon speaks of "good news" from a far country, and we have all experienced the joy of a stack of letters, eager anticipation of news from our loved ones. But there are times when we become the bearers of "bad news" to our co-workers, or we may be the recipients of bad news. How do we respond to those who are grieving or how do we give the news to another that a beloved family member or friend many miles away has died?

Our own experience often makes it easier to relate to others. A knock at our door was not unusual in itself, but the message shattered my world. So unexpectedly I heard those words, "Your mother died this afternoon." My first thought and reaction was denial. It's not true. It must be a mistake. She wasn't even sick. Hadn't I just received a letter from her that very day? Only as my husband looked at the telephone number we were instructed to call and found it was my parents' number and a co-worker (who had received the message of her father's death just six months before) kindly explained, "Yes, it is true your mother is dead," did it become reality. How I thanked God for the kindness of fellow workers and national believers as they helped pack suitcases and prepare clothes for our family of six to leave for the States. I felt appreciation for those who just sat and talked to me about my mother, and for several missionary families who met us at the airport the following morning to share their love and concern. God met my need at that moment by Christian brothers and sisters when my own blood brothers and sisters were many miles away!

It is important to break news gently, prepare the person(s) at least with the words "I have bad news for you," and give them a minute to prepare for the message. Stay with them; do not ask them what to do; just do whatever needs to be done—help them face reality, allow them to cry (tears are healing), and pray with them!

Rejoice with those who rejoice, and weep with those who weep!

Help!

READ: Matthew 10:1-8

She called one morning. I hadn't known her or even met her. Someone had told her about me, that maybe I could help. Her voice was desperate and she struggled to control her emotions.

"Please, can you help us? Our daughter is involved with evil powers. Strange things are happening in our house. She is not the same girl anymore. She says things and does things that are not her. But nobody believes us, not even our minister. Some tell us that this is normal for a young adolescent and that we should see a psychologist if we want help. Don't these people know this is the devil? Why can't these professionals help us?"

"Linda, we know this is real. The only thing that can help you and your daughter is the power of God and the blood of Jesus."

"Oh, thank you. You're the first person who's believed us. We would be so happy for any help you can give us. Can you come over?"

We prayed, pled the blood for protection, went, and ministered as God's Spirit led.

"Oh God, show us, Your people, how to minister to desperate people all around us. Show us how to care.

Move us with compassion. Teach us how to show love.

"Forgive us for not wanting to get involved, . . . especially in cases that are too difficult or too frightening. We can give so much advice, yet show so little compassion.

"Teach us in Your school how to minister grace. Get us out of our security boxes and release us from our selfishness. Open our hearts to receive others, as You've received us."

CHAPTER ELEVEN

"Here Am I; Send Me"
Isaiah 6:8

Who Will Go for Me?

READ: Romans 10:11-17

As I pick up our schoolchildren every afternoon and enjoy their chatter about their day, I wonder how many children in our community come home to an empty house. As I listen to our four teenagers share the highlights of their day, I wonder how the parents who came home and found that their fifteen-year-old son had committed suicide in their living room can face another day. As I listen to my youngsters play a game together, my heart aches for the many children who spend nearly all their spare time watching TV.

As I take my aging parents shopping or our family helps them cut their winter wood supply, I wish all the elderly in our community had someone who cares.

As I enjoy the security of a happy marriage, it saddens my heart to think of the many adulterous relationships which exist so close to us.

As I read my Bible each morning and pray for strength for the day, it burdens me to think that some church leaders tell their flock not to study the Word for themselves because they are not able to interpret it.

As I think of the price of my redemption, my heart bleeds for the many in our "Christian" nation who believe that eternal life is merited by good works. As I experience the miracle of a burden lifted or a grudge being removed, I long to tell someone, "I serve a living Saviour."

In our land of plenty, the welfare department provides physical needs but they have nothing to offer to the starving souls. They do not provide comfort for aching hearts. They do not provide companionship to the lonely.

May we cast our comfortable complacency aside and put on a not-so-comfortable concern for the lost with whom we come in contact. May we be observant of the opportunities to show them we care about their eternal destiny.

The Heart Call

READ: Matthew 9:35-38

"O God," I cried, "why may I not forget?
These halt and hurt in life's hard battle
Throng me yet.
Am I their keeper? Only I? To bear
This constant burden of their grief and care?
Why must I suffer for the others' sin?
Would God my eyes had never opened been!"
And the Thorn-crowned and Patient One
Replied, "They thronged Me too; I too have seen."

"But Lord, Thy other children go at will,"
I said, protesting still.
"They go, unheeding. But these sick and sad,
These blind and orphan, yes and those that sin
Drag at my heart. For them I serve and groan.
Why is it? Let me rest, Lord. I have tried—"
He turned and looked at me:
"But I have died!"

"But Lord, this ceaseless travail of my soul!
This stress! This often fruitless toil
These souls to win!
They are not mine: I brought not forth this host
Of needy creatures, struggling, tempest tossed,

They are not mine."
He looked at them—the look of One divine;
He turned and looked at me. "But they are mine!"

"O God," I said. "I understand at last.
Forgive! And henceforth I will bondslave be
To the least, weakest, vilest ones;
I would not more be free."
He smiled and said,
"It is to me."

—Lucy Rider Meyer

Relinquishment and Renewal

READ: Luke 5:1-11

The nerve of those men—to leave their boats (they had lots of hours and dollars invested in their crafts). The nerve to leave their equipment and gear (they were not listed as disposable yet). I wonder if the thought of public auction occurred to them. The church could've used the money. Or missions. Or Jesus. He didn't even SUGGEST selling out.

Peter, James, and John were men. Humans. So we should understand. Their fingers wouldn't have let go so easily if Jesus hadn't appeared to them. And if He wouldn't have given them such a manifestation of HIMSELF and His power.

But because they SAW Jesus, saw what He could do and who He is, and then saw themselves—"I am a sinful man" -they left everything. They knew they weren't the losers for it.

God, I've got my "boat and equipment and gear" too—
   my husband, our two daughters,
   my reputation, our plans, our future.
I ask for a manifestation of Your power in my life.
   I ask to see You,
   and then for loose fingers, unclenched hands
   to LET GO
and relinquish
   ALL;
and I know I won't be a loser.

274

Vision

READ: Joel 2:28-32

The world is wider
    than this mission field.
There are other horizons
    besides this one
    in this tiny corner
    of this small country.
There are other kitchen windows
    besides this one,
    through which other women
    view needy mankind passing.
There are other souls
    to pray for,
    other causes
    to work for,
    other churches
    to build,
    other spots besides
    this spot
    where the Lord
    has put me.
I'm happy here.
But I need the reminder:
I don't have the monopoly
    on other people's prayers,
    or their giving,
    or their interest.
Don't let me become narrow-minded, Lord!

Missionary Ethics

READ: Isaiah 58:6-12

I think—
 If I give you food,
 you will get hungry again.
 If I give you clothes,
 they will wear out.
 If I build you a better house,
 it will need to be repaired.
But God says—
 I am to do all these (Isaiah 58:7)
 and more besides.
 I must believe you were created in God's image
 as I was (Genesis 1:27)
 so that you will believe it too.
 I must treat you with respect
 as I want you to treat me (Luke 10:27)
 so that you will respect yourself.
 I must tell you about God who loves you
 as He loves me (I John 4:9)
 so that you will feel secure.
 I must share God's Good News with you
 as someone did with me (John 3:16, 17)
 so that you will believe and be saved.

—Author Unknown

What Is a Commitment?

READ: Hebrews 5:5-9

Commitment is to Jesus, the Son of God—not to myself, or to duty, or family, or church, or service.

—Commitment is taking my hands off my life and saying, "Lord Jesus, You take the reins."

—Commitment is coming to the mission field, sight unseen, and saying, "I'll stay."

—Commitment is staying when I want to run away.

—Commitment is loving when it is easier to resent or be bitter.

—Commitment is singing when I would rather pity myself.

—Commitment is taking time for important things, like having private devotions, giving my husband or child my attention, going to visit someone, planting flowers.

—Commitment is devotion to the Son of God and not simply devotion to His service.

—Commitment is staying up late to finish a letter to a loved one or a dress for a sister.

—Commitment is going out on midnight sick calls with a song—or at least not too much grumbling!

—Commitment is selling or giving away what is precious to me to help make good relationships.

—Commitment is mounting the guard of the Spirit at the door of my lips.

A commitment's rewards are varied: a smile exchanged,
a friendship built,
another Christian strengthened,
a lost soul saved and cleansed,
inner joy that my life pleases God and honors Him.

The crowning reward will be to hear Him say, "Well done, thou good and faithful servant."

A Real Live Missionary

READ: Isaiah 6:5-10

A real live missionary—our children always laughed as they listened to a story record and Aunt Teresa asked the question, "Did you ever see a real live missionary?"

Some time after we were living in the States again, I needed to have surgery. As the orderly wheeled me up to the O.R., I was shivering from the cold. Feeling a little frightened, I apologetically explained that we had lived in Central America for a number of years, and now I was always cold. Looking at me in amazement, he asked, "Were you a missionary?" When I replied affirmatively, he remarked, "This is the first time I ever spoke to a missionary!" My sister was waiting for me in my room when I came back from surgery and was surprised to hear the orderly instruct the nurses to take special care of this lady!

We smile, because we realize that missionaries are very ordinary people—traveling to another country doesn't cause instant transformation! Probably one of the biggest problems on the field is the missionary himself! Personality conflicts are the number one reason for missionaries returning prematurely to their home communities.

What does God have to say about this? In Isaiah 6:5, Isaiah confesses, "Woe is me! for I am undone." We, too, need to confess that we are human, selfish, and undone. We must ask God to make us fit vessels through which He can work and through which He will receive glory.

Missionaries, yes, live human beings who desire to share Christ with others!

279

Thoughts on Influence
READ: I Peter 3:8-16

Someone has said that one influences approximately one thousand people in his lifetime.

We who are blessed with daily door callers plus caring for our families have an especially wide ministry. Our words and actions become like pebbles dropped into a quiet pool of water which send out ever-widening ripples. Where do the ripples stop?

Doorkeeper

READ: Luke 18:28-30; Psalm 84:10

I was relatively new on the field and homesick. Being seven months pregnant didn't help things. Why couldn't we just go back home where things were as I was used to having them? Why did we have to be here where there were so many people but so few who even tried to understand? Back home there were our families and friends. There had been a caring and sharing church fellowship that was so distant now. Was this just the way missionary life was?

One day my husband listened to my woeful tales with a kindly ear and brought my attention to Luke 18:28-30. Those verses seemed to have escaped me in years gone by, and now as I read them, they were loaded with meaning. How wonderful that I was indeed receiving "manifold more in this **present** time." There were rewards—and not just on the eternal side. The weed of discontent had grown so tall in my heart that my eyes were blinded. Yes, I would rather be a "doorkeeper in the house of my God" than to be out of His will.

Without Him?—Failure

READ: John 15:1-8

As I try to do the task He has assigned, I realize I am getting nowhere. The deadline looms before me in big, bold letters. I can't think. My mind is full of little bits and pieces of things that don't fit together. Suddenly I am made aware of the fact that He is to do this work, not I. Perhaps there is so much of self in the way that I cannot hear God speaking.

I fall on my knees and ask Him to take the work in His hands. If He wants me to do it, He can provide words that are from Him, not words that make others think that I have the answer to everything.

Many times, as a minister's wife, I am called upon to teach a Sunday school class or answer a question someone may have. Perhaps someone comes to me for counsel for a problem they may be having. It seems people automatically suppose that ministers' wives have ready answers to so many of their questions. At times we may even have a tendency to think so ourselves. But we can be so thankful that God in His wisdom doesn't usually let us go on thinking that very long. He can give us a blank mind or humiliate us with a blunder and then we may be reminded of Psalm 127:1, "Except the Lord build the house, they labor in vain that build it."

Dear Lord, guide my thoughts today. May I totally depend on You as I do Your bidding. I want *You* to be seen and not *my* ideas and opinions.

Why Am I Here?

READ II Corinthians 5:10-21

My neighbor lady came to call one day. She wanted a needle. As we visited, our conversation turned to the subject of being a Christian. She had made a commitment once and then had given up. As we talked, I discovered she was very defensive. The message I got from her was, "Maybe everyone else is bad, but I have good reasons for my actions." I witnessed to her of her need to be saved, the coming judgment, etc. After she was gone, statements I had made to her insisted on coming back to me in the form of questions.

I told her we came because we wanted to help people here, including her and her family. Is that *really* why I'm here? Or is it because I like the lifestyle (sometimes!) or wanted to be close to my two sisters here or . . .?

Am I really concerned about her *soul*? Or am I more concerned about proving to her that I'm right and she's wrong?

And then the question of victory: I told her we don't need to live under sin anymore. Jesus makes it possible to "win over sin." I am not perfect, but I don't go sinning like I used to. Oh, don't I? Am I consistently victorious? And if not, why not? What happens to my testimony?

Searching questions, aren't they?

Prayer: "Search my heart, O Lord. Purify my motives. Recreate in me a warm, loving, gentle compassion for those among whom I live. For Jesus' sake, Amen·"

283

The Need at My Door

READ: Romans 14:7-12

She came to my door at times. I knew she had a need. We had talked about it, and she wanted to do right, but there were excuses. I had no idea how desperate her situation was.

She lived in a little village up on a hill almost a mile from my home. Hers was a humble cohune house with palm leaf roof and pole walls; a simple life of fixing tortillas, washing in the stream, and caring for her three children; a short life of 21 years.

She and her husband had stepped out to do right, but others had laughed and taunted. Discouragement set in and they gave up. She still seemed to have a degree of happiness but lacked true joy and peace.

Unknown to us, she was having difficulties with her mother-in-law, who lived close by. One evening she felt that she had had too much, and she mixed and drank a cup of poison. She never lived to see another sunset.

As I walked to her mother's home the next day before the burial, my heart was full of sorrow and anguished questioning. Had I done all that I could do for her? Were there times when I should have walked that mile to speak to her? Had I chafed at the time it took when she came to visit and my work was waiting?

But no more can I help her.

Now other needs come to my door. I must take time for them.

Limited Resources?

READ: James 1:5-8

It seems that as a missionary wife and mother I constantly struggle with priorities. I feel so pulled apart. All I ever get done is fix meals, wash clothes, sew, and clean the house—the bare necessities.

What about spending more time with the children? Our four-year-old recently began wetting her bed at night when her older sister started school. And our six-year-old has these absurd fears she pays attention to.

What about our church family back home? Other friends and family members need to hear from us so they can better pray for us. What about spending more time with my national sisters? And then there are our visitors to entertain and care for.

Humanly speaking there simply isn't enough time to do everything I "should" do. How would Jesus have handled the situation? Pat King writes about Jesus in her book, *How to Have All the Time You Need Every Day*.

"The Father had given Him a message to teach but He didn't have to search for people to listen. They sought Him out. He did not apologize for not curing or teaching the crowds while His physical body was being restored and refreshed. Jesus flowed with the hours of the day. He always had enough time."

"If any of you lack wisdom, let him ask of God . . ." (James 1:5a).

Handling Pressure

READ: Mark 3

Sometimes I seem to feel the walls of pressure pushing in all around me. There's so much to do and not enough time to do it. My husband and children, my co-workers, visitors, native Christians, and neighbors all need chunks of my time and resources. I'm spread thin and I don't reach.

Then I remember Jesus. He experienced much more pressure than I do. In today's Scripture reading we see the many different kinds of pressure our Lord faced: crowds of people, Satanic attack, overwhelming workload, demands of others, criticism, opposition, family misunderstandings.

How did He react? He didn't get uptight or irritable. He didn't snap at people or go to pieces. Jesus responded with compassion.

Help me, Lord, to learn of You.

Be Not Weary

READ: Galatians 6:7-10

Life on the mission field is wearing. You often feel so draggy and uninspired. Tiredness becomes a way of life.

Even then, "Let us not be weary in well doing."

—When you don't want to see another person at your door.

—When the demands of your children are seemingly endless.

·When you long for rest; some quiet, uninterrupted place apart.

Be not weary! Breathe a prayer and find your strength for the moment in Jesus' compassion for others.

"For in due season we shall reap, if we faint not."

But there are so many going their own way,
so many interested but not committed,
so many Christians easily discouraged.

Keep on in welldoing; there will be fruit.

You may not see it now, for that is in God's time.

Trust in God—the harvest time will come.

When the weary days, the tiredness, the daily welldoing are past, your welcome rest shall come with soothing words, "Well done, enter thou into the joy of thy Lord."

Accomplishments or Position?

READ: Luke 10:1-20

My days were filled to the brim as a missionary wife and mother of five. I taught Sunday school, ladies' Bible study, and Wednesday evening children's class. There were many local callers and other visitors to be entertained. I was happy and fulfilled and in the secret of my heart, I'm sure I felt quite indispensable.

But then it happened. On a cold, sub-zero day in January, I needed to take a very sick lady to the hospital. On my way home I picked up our three sons from school. Suddenly, a pickup truck passed me on the slippery road. The car coming toward me swerved into my lane and we collided head-on. No one else in my car was seriously hurt, but I was taken to the hospital with a cracked vertebra and other injuries. There I stayed for thirty-two days.

Now other people did all those things I had been doing! Friends brought in meals for my family and did the laundry. One lady fixed school lunches for our three boys.

And what was the Lord teaching me? Suddenly I wasn't *doing* anything! Just lying on my back, unable at first even to lift my head from the pillow. I knew the Lord was with me and I felt His presence in a real way. But as the days and weeks went by, I became discouraged and depressed about being so helpless and wondered how long it would be until I would be well again.

One day I was reading in Luke 10 about the seventy disciples coming back to Jesus and telling Him about the wonderful things that were happening. Jesus' words in verse 20 spoke directly to my heart. He seemed to be saying to me, "Rejoice in your *position*, not in your accomplishments." And I understood that the basis for me being a happy and fulfilled person does not lie in me doing many good things, but in knowing that my name is in the records of heaven!

Did I Finish the Work?

READ: Mark 14:3-9

At the close of today, what do I see accomplished? It's a good feeling to have the patching done, the wash folded and put away, or some baking done ahead. But the better feeling is to look back on a busy day without regret. How much I want to level that mountain of patching! But I must not upset my household in order to complete the task. These earthly things won't matter "tomorrow" so I must not let them matter too much today.

Did I finish the work God gave me to do today? The work of caring, of showing kindness, of praying, of listening, of instructing . . . interwoven with the cooking, cleaning, washing.

At the close of my life, will I have finished the work God gave me to do? If daily I am faithful in doing this work, then yes will be the answer in the end.

On Giving and Receiving

READ: Luke 6:34-38

We are on furlough. Gracious hospitality, wonderful meals, and late-night visits with dear friends are thoroughly enjoyed. We accept the special gifts to take back with us—fluffy new bath towels, a quilt, fabric for a dress, a bag of precious walnuts, maple syrup, Velveeta cheese, and new games. And we know they will continue financial and prayer support as we return to our place of service. With deep gratefulness we accept their generosity and determine to be faithful servants of the Lord.

But as we leave, a nagging thought persists. How can we repay them for all they are doing for us? What can we give them in return? Is there something we can do for them?

But wait, what did Jesus teach about this? He said, "Freely ye have received, freely give" (Matt. 10:8b). Jesus also asked what reward we have if we give only to people that we hope to receive from again (Luke 6:34). Most of the time there will be no need to give back to the same people who give to us. This frees us to give wherever we see a need. And the chain of giving can go on from one person to the next as there is need.

Then . . . back to the field in Canada again.

Children come to the door for a drink of water. A boy wants to use the tire pump. A poor man asks for a sandwich. Someone wants to use the phone. You play a game of Uno with a lonely child. Two hours of a busy morning are spent listening to and encouraging a frustrated mother. You teach Sunday school every quarter, year after year.

"Thank You, Lord, for the privilege of receiving . . . and giving wherever and whenever there is a need."

Mary With "Much Serving"

READ: Luke 10:38-42

Lord, "the people" throng me. My work in the kitchen multiplies. I long to be a "Mary" having quiet times of meditation and relaxation, but I find myself a busy "Martha."

But my story can be different from the one about Martha who was cumbered with much serving. Lord, You have given me the "much serving" to do. I didn't and wouldn't ask for it.

Yet I can be a "Mary" through the day. Your presence is within me, and I can talk with You and hear You speak to me as Bible verses come to my mind or I feel conviction for an unkind word. Then, too, I can feel compassion for the many needy souls and pray for them. I can learn kindness and patience and show Your love to others.

And then, in my special time set apart in the day, I shall be a Mary. In a quiet corner, I shall have my time alone with You. In reading Your Word and meditating and praying, I will experience more fully that "better part" and shall go forth refreshed to the "much serving" that awaits me.

293

Housewife or Homemaker?

READ: Psalm 34:11-22

Have you ever heard the expression, "Oh, I'm just a housewife"? I don't think I have ever said it, but I *have* felt that way. What a pitiable state to be in—married to a house and all the work it involves.

Once a man was interviewing us and he asked me about my vocation.

I replied, "I'm a homemaker."

"Oh," he responded, unimpressed. Then in his neat little blank, he wrote (you guessed it) "housewife."

At a missionaries' meeting we were encouraged to list what we do for a whole week, keeping record by fifteen-minute slots. I tried it and learned a number of things before the week was over.

First, I decided a list is helpful in discerning just what consumes all my time.

Second, by the looks of the chart I *am* a housewife! What else do you call a person who spends over half her waking hours feeding and clothing bodies and cleaning their dwelling place?

Third, a chart does not tell you if you are a homemaker. It doesn't say things such as "I grouched at David," or, "I rejoiced with Jonathan when he found his lost ball." It doesn't say, "I was really perturbed that our neighbor came walking right into

294

the house without even announcing his presence," or, "I found it a pleasure to help Regina find information for her report." Neither does it say, "I fell asleep when I was praying," in my time slot marked "devotions."

The things that make a home are not what I do with my hands, but what I do with my attitudes.

Today I choose. Will I be just a housewife or will I make a home?

Who Am I?

READ: John 13:1-17

I am a *Helpmeet* to my husband. I stand beside him ready to encourage him, assist him, love him, and even at times to relinquish him for the sake of others.

I am a *Mother,* meeting the needs of my children just the same as any other mother, except with being in a foreign land, my children's needs may be different and sometimes more demanding because of the influence of ungodly playmates, infections, etc.

I am a *Homemaker,* learning to cook in a new culture with new foods, no modern conveniences, water to boil, visitors to feed and entertain.

I am a *Substitute Mother,* a big sister to the V.S. workers—dealing with their homesickness, frustrations, and questions.

I am a *Friend* to the village mothers, learning from them and also teaching them by word and example.

Sometimes I feel like my work is unnoticed and unappreciated. I miss out on the excitement, the adventure of my husband or the single worker. Then I remember that Jesus washed the disciples' feet. He came not to be ministered unto, but to minister and I rejoice that—

I am a *Servant* and gladly will I serve my husband, my family, and anyone God brings into my life!

296

A New World

READ: I Peter 4:12-16

As the plane was preparing to land, I hastily scribbled a few more lines to the letter I was writing to my parents, with the words, "It feels like we're entering a new world. Please pray for us!" It certainly did feel like a new world to my husband and me and our two little boys, as we entered a country, a culture we had never seen before and knew very little about!

As we left the plane, we immediately were aware of the stifling heat and humidity, the warmest time of the year when the butter melts simply sitting on the table. Strange faces greeted us at the airport, and we struggled to keep up with the complete newness and changes facing us in the new world.

Many years have passed since that day. Those little boys are now grown men who are already facing new challenges and life on their own, and I reflect on advice I can share with those who are facing the new unknown world, especially on other soil in another culture. I would say first and foremost:

Give yourself time to adjust. You will feel differently in a week, a month or a year. Don't compare yourself with those who have been there longer, or the one you are replacing. Expect a culture shock, and allow yourself time to get over it. You can expect to be homesick, but this too will pass!

Accept the people you have come to minister to. You are prepared to teach them. You have a lot to offer them. But they are going to teach you more! Be teachable—their way may be better than you think! Ask them for help. Let them show you how things are done in this new land. Your culture needs to remain in your country, and let their culture rub off on you (unless it violates godly principles).

Remember, you are the stranger, the uninvited guest in their country and even in their village. We sometimes expect people automatically to appreciate us for the "sacrifice" we've made to help them, but it doesn't always work that way! We may be misunderstood and unappreciated. Jesus was too!

Adjusting

READ: John 12:20-26

New on the mission field. Adjusting. Everyone else knows what they are doing. I don't. I feel useless. Bewildered. "Commit thy works unto the Lord, and thy thoughts shall be established," not bewildered.

I make so many mistakes. The Kekchis are so quiet. I am uncomfortably loud. Their strange customs make me grope for the security of the familiar. "Lean not unto thine own understanding." Learn how they think.

The old me is dying. May the new me emerge totally dependent on God. A corn of wheat that falls in the ground and dies brings forth much fruit.

First Furlough

READ: Philippians 1:22-30

Anticipation:
—days of waiting; will it ever come?
Excitement:
—the plane ride, reunion at the airport, tears, hugs, and kisses!
Joy:
—being at home base again with family and friends.

Perhaps we're not prepared for a
Critical Spirit:
—do people really need all those extras, carpets on the floor, beautiful dishes, expensive clothes, rich foods? If they could only see how other people live!
The Pedestal Experience:
—we are the missionaries, but we feel so human, burned out. Our clothes suddenly look old and shabby. *Please,* just treat us like ordinary people!
Frustration:
—dinner invitations, speaking engagements, the children begging to go home.
Anticipation:
—packing the suitcase to return. What more can we get in? Only two more nights to sleep!
Joy:
—home again, in the place where God has called us, with a new desire to give our best to this corner of God's vineyard!

Time Apart

READ: Psalm 84

Furlough time is coming up and we're looking forward to being with family and friends in familiar places. We're excited about traveling and taking in meetings, and we're anticipating the rest from the demanding routine here.

But we're also remembering other furlough times with our over-full schedules, trying to get around to see "everyone" and finding it impossible, long shopping lists, tired children who feel it that they're not at home. In short, those times can be just as demanding, though different.

So we have some goals.

We want to absorb all the blessings we can in church services and meetings. We want to visit friends. (We remember the blessings of fellowship that lingered after we got home last time.) But we don't want to wear out dashing from place to place for meals or filling up every night of the week with going somewhere. We plan to limit our going and still make the most of times of fellowship.

We hope to do some special things as a family: spend time in the mountains, pick peas in Grandma's garden, and pick cherries in the orchard.

We'd like to see the shopping done as soon as

possible. It's more relaxing to have the shopping list whittled down in a hurry.

We aim to have our quiet times of Bible reading and prayer. It's easy to neglect this away from home and ordinary routine.

As furlough time is a break between terms of service, we will be evaluating the past years and seeing areas needing change or growth in the future. We hope to return with renewed determination, commitment, and zeal gleaned from the fellowship, meditation, and rest in this time apart and away.

Contentment on Furlough?
READ: Hebrews 13:5-9

You thought you were going home. Now you feel like a stranger in your own country. You expected furlough to be a vacation, but the demands on your time and privacy are greater than they were on the field. You were eager to hear someone else for a change, but everywhere you go, your husband is asked to preach.

Everything's so different, so clean, so beautiful. Instead of stark poverty, you encounter affluence. You see big cars on big highways, big tables loaded with big dishes of rich food, big lawnmowers on big lawns by big houses. But most impressive are the big garbage cans.

You've suddenly gone from being a rich foreigner to being a poor missionary. Instead of giving, you are now receiving. Feeling useless, you recognize the truth of Jesus' words, "It is more blessed to give than to receive."

Friends and relatives clamor for time with you. You feel spread thin and pulled apart. People in your home church know and recognize you. You feel guilty because you can't remember their names. You feel unworthy of their respect and admiration.

Your children's table manners embarrass you. You

hadn't realized that they had become so "bushed." They turn up their noses at the strange food. You hope your hosts don't notice.

Culture shock gives way to feelings of unreality, feelings of being disconnected. Which is the real world, this one or the one you just left? Or are they both real?

How, you wonder, could you be homesick at home? Now you realize that "home" is the land you left behind when you went on furlough.

Paul learned to be content in any situation. Contentment doesn't come automatically or naturally. It's learned.

For many missionaries, it's hard to be content on furlough. It helps to look around for ways to serve. People everywhere need encouragement, a smile, a word of cheer. Contentment can be found in service.

With practice, if we try hard, we can learn to be content, even on furlough.

Prayer for Furlough Mothers

READ: Psalm 16

May God give you
... wisdom
> to keep your priorities straight, so that you take time alone with the Lord. It is so easy to neglect that vital time in the rush of going and the excitement of doing.

... understanding and love
> to be the wife your husband needs when it seems like everyone else is getting more of his attention than you are, and you thought this was going to be your time to be together a lot.

... calmness
> when the children require even more mothering than in the "bush." Sometimes it seems like it takes so long for them to get adjusted.

... a forgiving spirit
> toward friends who don't understand you or your husband. There are times when those we expected to understand us best understand us least. May He help you remember that they have not shared all your growth, struggles, and re-evaluation of life. (Jesus' nearest disciples misunderstood Him.)

... a gracious spirit
> in living with your family and your in-laws.

May He bless you with
- ... an attitude of gratitude for the smallest favor shown or the most unwanted gift.
- ... the joy of sharing with other mothers.
- ... the fellowship of your many friends.
- ... the excitement of seeing new things through your children's eyes.
- ... the wisdom (and fun) in shopping.
- ... and the desire to return to His place of service for you.

Where He Leads

READ: Exodus 13:20-22; Psalm 32:8

Sometimes missionaries face the decision as to when to leave the field. Sometimes it is easier than others. Our decision was based on a problem we faced while serving on the foreign field. Although it was hard for us to understand, we definitely felt that God was telling us to return to the States.

We followed His direction and were amazed how everything seemed to work out for our good. It was like a jigsaw puzzle. Everything fell into place perfectly.

I was reminded of the Israelites who had a pillar of cloud by day and one of fire by night to lead wherever God chose. It is comforting to know that God still leads us today if we are willing to follow!

"For this God is our God for ever and ever: he will be our guide even unto death" (Psalm 48:14).

Good-Bye

READ: Philippians 2:13-16

It's another beautiful morning in Belize. Warm. Birds singing. Chickens cackling. Everything outside seems usual. But this Sunday is different from all the rest—it's our last one as residents, and I'm asking myself some heart-searching questions. Will the people in this village remember me as being a kind and loving person, one who was willing to help? Or will they best remember me as cynical and sarcastic?

Scene after scene appears in my mind's eye as I review the past years—some good, some not so good. "Oh, why was I so impatient? So uncaring and unfeeling? When will I learn to say no in a kind way?"

"Lord, forgive me . . . and change me. Help me remember how crowds thronged You when here on earth. Yet Your attitudes were always right, even when You were weary! Help me remember that every person coming to my door has a never-dying soul and You are most pleased when I respond accordingly."

Reentry

READ: Colossians 4:8-13

A few months after returning to the States, we attended a farewell service for a missionary family who were returning to the field. Afterward a friend remarked to me that I could probably really sympathize with the missionary family. I was at a loss for words—my tears had been for myself! I wanted to be the one returning, going home, again!

Friends and family will care about us and pray for us when we leave for the field, but they can't quite understand the frustrations when we come back. They expect us to be glad to be home again. But is this home to children who have been born in another country or have lived there for a long time? Our children may go through a real culture shock—everything is so new, so different! Adjusting to a new school system can be very difficult. Small things like using a clean sheet of paper for every subject, when they had been taught to save paper! Language problems, a different accent may make them feel self-conscious! New friends, they don't want to be treated like "missionary children," but want to feel accepted like everyone else!

Financial problems become a large frustration—needing to equip a whole family with winter clothes (thank God for the blessings of Goodwill Stores and friends who share). Even so, there are times when there is no money to buy groceries, and we must simply trust God to meet our needs!

It is very important to guard against critical attitudes—wrong attitudes cause bitterness! As we find our place again in the home community, we learn to continue reaching out to those around us and discover there are many people with physical and spiritual needs, waiting at our doorsteps!

Let's bloom where we are planted, whether in a foreign country or in the States!

310

CHAPTER TWELVE

"Gather Up The Fragments That Remain"
John 6:12

Tune In

READ: Psalm 88:1-13

Dear Father,

This two-meter radio hasn't worked right for months.

I'm weary of trying to talk and not being heard. The voices of others come in clearly. My fellow workers are very patient with my ability to give only one beep for *no* and two for *yes*.

Since the first weeks I queried what lesson You wanted to teach me. Did You want me to quit talking so much? Or did You want to quench my communication with others and quicken my communion with You?

Lately I hear You whisper, "Now you know how I feel." Maybe I do in part. Is this how You feel when I come running to You with a question and give You a multiple-choice answer and none of them is *Your* answer? But I am not in tune enough to hear what Your answer is. Or is this how You feel when a sister and I discuss a problem but we don't have any answers? All the while You know the solution but we haven't thought to ask You.

Sometimes I'm quiet all day. I bring nothing to You, no thanks, no praise, no requests, just no turning to You because You don't answer audibly anyway. Surely You long for fellowship.

Other people listen to You when they pray. I don't know how to do that. Will You teach me? My hurrying, sleepiness, and yes, plain laziness keep me from listening or even praying.

For the praise of Your glory I ask it.

Amen.

Mary or Martha?

READ: Luke 12:13-21

Did you ever wonder whether you are a Mary or a Martha? Answer the following questions carefully and honestly to discover your own priorities.

1. Do I a.) take time to sit at Jesus' feet each day?
   b.) rush right into the temporal duties without a thought of needing Him?
2. Do I a.) listen to Him speak in a still, small voice?
   b.) fill my life so full of (good) activities that the only time I can hear God is if He speaks in a disaster?
3. When uncontrollable circumstances arise, do I
   a.) rest in Him?
   b.) become frustrated and encumbered with the thought of what could happen?
4. Do I a.) care more about my relationship with my husband and family?
   b.) care more about a spotless house, a good book, or a hobby?
5. Do I cook as though I a.) eat to live?
   b.) live to eat?
6. Am I more concerned about my child's
   a.) spiritual health?
   b.) physical health?

7. Is helping others a
     a.) blessing to me?
     b.) burden to me?
8. Do I a.) find time to visit the widows and lonely shut-ins?
     b.) use all my extra time for the things that have no eternal value?
9. As the world views my life, would they
     a.) realize I am seeking a better country?
     b.) have reason to think I plan to stay here forever?
10. Do I a.) know God?
     b.) know about God?

Poster Message or a Screaming Poster?

READ: I Timothy 6:6-12

The entire time we were on the mission field a certain poster hung on our bathroom wall. I never thought the picture was pretty, but there were times the words fairly screamed at me!

In the early days when I was experiencing adjustment and growing pains (wondering why we ever came in the first place), I often came to the bathroom to cry. There were numerous other occasions when it would jump out at me at just such times to minister, bringing healing and growth.

The poster said, "Happiness is not having what you want, but wanting what you have!" Gradually it dawned on me that if I wasn't content with what I have *now*, I probably never would be.

Since our return home, an equally heavy reminder has become a part of my life: "To be content with little is hard; to be content with much is impossible!"

The Apostle Paul said, "I have learned, in whatsoever state I am, therewith to be content" (Philippians 4:11). But . . . why can't I learn?

315

Abnormal Living

READ: II Samuel 22:29-37

Many of us have problems with what we call "abnormal living." Our idea of a normal life and our life situations are two different things. So we have a hard time handling life as it comes to us. Life isn't what we had pictured, and we "fight" it in our minds.

If we are where God wants us to be and these are the circumstances that come along with being in His will, we had better start calling them something besides abnormal. The portion that God has for you in life is not abnormal. It is His choice and His best for you. In trials, God does not "afflict willingly." He has holy purpose in what He does and allows.

That does not change the circumstances, but with a heart change and a mind change, rather than bracing yourself and fighting against situations, you will find them workable.

I love to think that God appoints
My portion day by day.
Events of life are in His hand,
And I would only say,
"Appoint them in Thine own good time
And in Thine own best way."

—A. L. Waring

Opportunities, Part I

READ: Luke 2:1-7; 19:28-38

The innkeeper had an opportunity to share a room with the Lord of glory. He missed it! He saw only a tired little woman and her poor husband.

The donkey owner had an opportunity to share a precious colt with the Lord of glory. He took it! He saw beyond the two rough disciples whose only explanation was, "The Lord has need."

Lord, how many times have You come to me with a need, and I saw only a dirty little child, an unmannerly man, a demanding woman? Not only at this Christmas season, but at all times let me be a donkey owner, in spite of *who* You send to ask, or *what* You ask for.

Opportunities, Part II

READ: II Corinthians 9:6-15

I really thought I was the donkey owner! But I didn't expect the Lord to test me and show me who I really was—the innkeeper! Did He really expect me to fry half a chicken for Him, or give Him my prettiest cloth (I couldn't wait to make a dress from it) or ask me for my last bit of precious peanut butter, or ask me on my busiest day to show Him how to sew pants, or ask me for my broom and not return it? What a lot of opportunities.

Lord, You know I gave, but grudgingly, not cheerfully; sparingly, not wholeheartedly. Lord, will you give me another opportunity to give without murmuring . . . to give with glad abandon?

Responsibility or Privilege?

READ: Colossians 3:18-24

Responsibility is a heavy word. It brings to mind pictures of a load or burden. And truly our responsibilities are heavy. We have our place to fill faithfully in the home. We need to be companions to our husbands, mothers to our children, friends to those who come to our houses The demands of our roles come thick and fast, and so often we feel that we are not fulfilling our responsibilities We just can't. It's "just too much ' and we're so bogged down under the weight of "responsibility." "We don't have what it takes," we tell ourselves and then complain at our husbands, scold our children, and force a smile at our callers.

Did you ever think of your responsibilities as God-given privileges and opportunities? Try it! It makes such a difference. Consider the *privilege* of sharing life with your husband; the *opportunity* of teaching and leading little ones; the privilege of sharing Christ's love with those who call. It takes the drudgery out of serving and gives life a propelling power.

Oh! The joy of privilege and opportunity!

Day After Day

READ: Psalm 71:1-14

Did you ever wish the cookie jar would stay filled, the laundry would stay done, or your tidy kitchen would never get messy again?

Jesus said, "Come unto me, all ye that labour and are heavy laden, and I will give you rest" (Matthew 11:28). How many times I need to flee to Him for rest. He keeps giving it to me again and again. He has never reprimanded me about my repeated requests for strength to fulfill the task ahead, as I sometimes do the children when the cookie jar is empty. He has never harshly asked me why the supply of grace He gave me yesterday isn't enough for today, as I did when my teenage son asked me for more clean socks. Jesus has never sighed in despair after He helped me out of one predicament only to find me sinking into another one, as I did Saturday morning when the girls had little bits of various cookie ingredients scattered all over my tidy kitchen.

I want to be more like Him in the repetitious duties of the home. And remember how many times He has supplied the same need for me day after day.

A List—Help or Hindrance?

READ: Luke 12:41-44; James 4:13-17; Proverbs 19:21

I am a list person. I make shopping lists, work lists, goal lists, and fix-it lists. If I plan to be gone a few hours, I make a list for the girls so they don't argue about who is to do what. Lists certainly free my mind from having to remember so many small things, but at the same time they can become a slave driver if I let them. If the things I put on my lists cause me to become irritated when I can't cross them all out, they are too important to me.

Jesus said of the woman who anointed His feet with expensive ointment, "She hath done what she could." He said of the poor widow who cast in two mites, "She has given all she had."

So often I put things on my list which I can't accomplish. The hours of a day just don't stretch that far, or God brings unexpected happenings into my day and the list is completely ignored.

Lord, grant me wisdom in making my lists that the intents of my heart may be to please You, not self. Open my eyes that I may see the most important things I must do and the strength to do them in that order. Free my mind of worrying about what others think if I'm not able to accomplish all that other sisters do, and give me rest as I allow *You* to take control of my lists.

Frustration or Fulfillment?

READ: Romans 12:1-8

Sources of Frustration:
Feelings of failure,
Relationship problems,
Unrealistic expectations,
Selfishness and pride,
Trouble understanding the language and culture
Resentments,
Anxiety about what others think,
Too little privacy,
Irritations, interruptions, inconveniences,
   intrusions,
Overwhelming responsibilities,
Not enough time with God.

Steps to Fulfillment:
Forgive and forget.
Understand your role.
List your priorities.
Find time for family fun.
Ignore what critics say about your husband.
Learn to substitute.
Laugh.
Maintain the integrity of your own person.
Entertain as unto Christ.
Never pity your children for being missionary
   children.
Thank God that you're a missionary wife.

Whose Money Do I Spend?

READ: II Corinthians 8:11-21

"How does it feel to be spending other people's money?" a visitor asked me. The question took me by surprise and aroused defensive feelings within me. I wondered, "Is this *really* the way our supporters feel? That we are spending *their* money!" Somehow I had come to accept our monthly allowance and the fringe benefits of housing and transportation as God's way of providing for our needs, just as any wage earner has his needs met by what he works! Up to this time I had never felt guilty or in need of defending the arrangement for our support.

So I turned to the Scriptures to see what God has to say about the matter. What an interesting study this was! I found out that the priests were to have their share of the meat, vegetables, and fleece (for clothes?) that the people brought for sacrifices (Deuteronomy 18:3-5). When Jesus sent out the 70 disciples, He assured them their physical needs would be met (Luke 10:7). He quoted the Old Testament Scripture, "The labourer is worthy of his hire." Paul, that great pioneer missionary, also gave some valuable insight. He was very concerned that the money that was donated by the churches be used in an honest and blameless way (II Corinthians 8:20, 21). For some reason, Paul accepted aid from some churches for his personal needs but not from others (II Corinthians 11:9). According to Acts 18:3, Paul was a tentmaker and worked part-time to support himself.

I am glad our visitor asked this probing question! Now I am assured that it is all right to have our financial needs met by the supporting churches. I am also more aware that we *are* responsible for the way we spend "their" money, and we always want to appreciate it and not take it for granted.

When I Fall

READ: Psalm 32

Someone once shared this thought with me: Every Christian is either in a standing position or else in a position to stand up.

I have been in situations where I suddenly realize I am very much out of the will of my Lord. Feelings of guilt and terrible failure engulf me. I have found the Lord to be very gracious in times like that. When I repent and confess my sin, He generously and lovingly forgives and restores peace and joy to my heart. Then I can stand again and be in His will and do His will right where I am. Doing His will may mean changing what I am doing in that particular setting. It may mean confessing to a person. It may mean changing my attitudes. But it is a blessing to know that when I inadvertently fall, God extends His grace to me so I can get up again right there.

"For a just man falleth seven times, and riseth up again" (Proverbs 24:16). "Though he fall, he shall not be utterly cast down: for the Lord upholdeth him with his hand" (Psalm 37:24).

P.S. The Lord wants me to extend this same gracious love to others.

Mountain Climbing

READ: Psalm 124

Women's sewing circle day leaves me exhausted both physically and emotionally. Since our house is built nine feet off the ground and our sewing room is in another building, the shortest route from my kitchen to the sewing room is down the back steps, to the left, through the gate, across the muddy lane, past the workshop, past the water vat, up three steps, and there you are. A needle, three buttons, a pattern, scissors, another bobbin—the list of the women's needs seems endless. Interruptions in this whole day of women's sewing circle seem to be the rule rather than the exception. So I am usually ready to collapse by the time I get everything cleaned up, put away, and carried back to the house. However, upon reaching the privacy of my own home, a new set of needs descends upon me! There is my husband and dear neglected children to consider and prepare supper for.

One particular sewing circle day we planned to have visitors for breakfast because it just didn't work out otherwise. I felt as though I was being asked to climb a mountain too big for me. During my quiet time that morning, I was inspired to look up verses on help. I found and recorded ten or twelve passages and received strength to tackle my duties head-on and with a lighter heart.

A Lesson on Dependence

READ: Proverbs 16:1-20; Isaiah 30:15; Psalm 37:5

I needed another lesson on dependence. As usual it was a painful one.

I got out of bed in the morning with my mind filled to the brim with the many things I needed to do. I was to take hot lunch to school. There was sewing circle. Daniel had a dentist appointment. And I really should have squeezed in time to take Kristina to the doctor after school to have the sores in her mouth checked out. Mechanically, I went through the motions of having devotions. I arose from prayer and hurried to get the children off to school so I could start the activities of the day. The more I hurried, the farther behind I got. At last I was almost ready to leave to take the lunch to the school and then go on to sewing circle. I glanced at the clock and then at the sink full of dirty dishes. They would just have to wait. How I hated days like this!

Questions began to plague my mind. "Is this God's plan for my day? Does He really get any honor and glory when my schedule is so crowded? What can I eliminate from my schedule today?" I decided Daniel's dentist appointment could be put off until another day. Quickly I phoned in and canceled the appointment. I also began to realize that my anxiety was coming from not entrusting this day to the Lord in the first place and from not looking to Him for my strength.

After much struggle, a few quiet moments with the Lord, some tears of relief, and a few encouraging words from my husband, I left, knowing, "This is the day which the Lord hath made; we will rejoice and be glad in it" (Psalm 118:24).

Gifts

READ: I Corinthians 15:8-11; Ephesians 4:12

God gave me gifts to serve Him. I became so enthralled with my gifts and involved in serving that He had to take my service away from me so I would look at Jesus.

Seeing Jesus, I see myself, His blundering servant,
    who needs to learn so much more about the Giver.

Seeing Him, I find He is all I need.

    What, then, are gifts?

Seeing Him teaches me how to better use the gifts
    He has given.

    And why to use them: obedience, not an ego trip.

If I am upset when I see my work questioned, misunderstood, mocked, destroyed

    —or given to another—

then Jesus is not my first love.

It is good He takes "my ministry" from me at times, so I can more clearly see my Jesus.

329

God's Ideal

READ: Isaiah 55:8-13

I used to think (still do sometimes!) that the ideal situation is where everything falls into place just like that—no waiting, no interruptions, no tears, no flat tires, etc.

One day God revealed this beautiful and very obvious truth to me. What we consider to be an ideal situation may be limited to the present and the passing. God's standard of ideal, however, is based upon the enduring and the eternal. In His eyes, an ideal situation is one in which we grow in Christ-like qualities such as patience, faith, and kindness. He arranges situations for us to exercise our spiritual muscles in developing these graces.

"Wherefore gird up the loins of your mind" (I Peter 1:13). Let us rise to the challenge.

If Walls Could Speak

READ: Proverbs 15

If the walls that house your family
  Could speak everything they know—
All the secrets you supposed
  Were hidden from all human souls.
Would you hope they would forget about
  The ugly words you uttered,
When someone crossed your path today
  Because you had it cluttered?

Would they cringe at harsh unkindnesses,
  And those slanderous remarks,
Which give the wedge another tap
  And split us far apart?
Or would the walls in your abode
  Say, "Those who dwell inside
Must truly love each other more
  Than self: for they are kind"?

Friend, walls can't hear, nor can they speak,
  But one in heaven knows
Each deed that's done, each uttered word
  Behind the well-kept doors.
When life is past and we stand before
  The Judge who hears each word,
We want to hear, "Well done, my child.
  Enter here—My joyful abode."

Between Thee and Him Alone

READ: Matthew 18:15-20

Answering a knock on my door, I let in a woman who had begun to rail at me even before she entered my house. She was upset at something I was supposed to have said to her mother the evening before.

Remembering the advice in Proverbs 15:1 about a soft answer turning away wrath, I tried to calm her down and get to the root of the problem.

Yes, I told her that, and no, that is not what I meant. No, I did not say that at all. Slowly we sorted fact from imagination. I was hurt by the accusation but was glad she had come straight to me instead of spreading tales about it to others. That would have hurt more.

When she left, she was in a different state of mind. She thanked me for my time and was glad to have the misunderstanding straightened out.

Her coming was in harmony with Matthew 18, even though her method might have been harsh. Here was someone who was not serving the Lord, and yet taking this approach. I was put to shame. Do I employ this method? Or do I spread problems to third parties first?

Who Is Being Rejected?

READ: John 15:18-27

None of us likes to be rejected. When we started to school, we wanted to have close friends. As a teenager, it was important to be accepted into our peer group. Later we hoped someone would love us enough to marry us. We wanted to be accepted for who we were and what we had to offer.

When we present the Gospel to people, we want them to accept what we have, too. And when they don't, we sometimes take it as a personal rejection.

Soon after we moved to Hudson, I went to visit two old ladies one day. I was hardly seated until I realized they had been drinking. Immediately one of them lashed out at me concerning a dream she had. "The Lord told me not to listen to the missionaries but to stick to my own religion!" she screamed again and again. There I sat, crushed in my spirit and tears stinging my eyes. Here were two ladies who we thought were open to the Gospel, and now one of them had had this dream to affirm her rejection of the truth. I felt deeply rejected.

As I sat there, I thought of the Lord's words to Samuel concerning the children of Israel. "They have not rejected thee, but they have rejected me" (I Samuel 8:7). I read the passage when I came home and prayed that the Lord would give me love and a forgiving heart. And if they kept on rejecting the Gospel, I wanted to remember it was the Lord they were rejecting and not me personally.

But It Is You,
My Close Friend

READ: Psalm 55

We hadn't talked together for long months.
We, who had often shared thoughts in Sunday school
    class.
We, who had prayed together and
    encouraged each other in witnessing.
We, who had wept together when my precious child
    was killed.

I went to see her.
I longed to share with her.
But she avoided me, answering my questions very
briefly, escaping outside while I visited with her
daughter.

With heavy heart I went to her.
I hugged her.
I told her I loved her and
    missed her very much.
I told her I pray for her every day.
I was close to tears . . .
    tears for my lack of overflowing love in former days.

She bent down and
    lifting the corner of her skirt,
    wiped the tears from her eyes.
She said nothing.
Did she understand the yearning I felt toward her?

334

This ugly rift—
Will it be here for years?
Will we ever be together again?
In heaven?
Why must we have these vicious church divisions,
    splits, splinters, and sides?

Why must families and friends be painfully severed?
Because of sin?
Whose sin?
Who is deceived?
Is it their side?
Or could it be ours?
The questions parade through my mind on their
    merry-go-round.

Can I have peace in the midst of divisions?
Yes.
Instead of defending the truth, I must live the truth.
The truth is love.
Love speaks no evil,
    no, more,
    thinks no evil.
Love looks not at their peculiarities
    but at their possibilities.
Love puts the best construction on their every action.
Love does not defend my own reputation
    or rights.
Love is kindness.
I ask not, "Lord, who is right?"
    but, "Lord, let me live the truth."

Grace Enough

READ: Romans 8:35-39

Last night while we were sleeping, someone tried to break in our back door. We knew there had been someone around, but not till we saw the marks at OUR back door did we realize that he had tried our house too! What did he want? Did he actually think he could sneak past our open bedroom door without us hearing him? Did he have a gun? Did he have rape in mind? No one has ever tried to get in while we were in the house before. And I'd always thought that as long as intruders didn't come in while we were at home I'd be safe. Now that security was taken away. All my defenses seemed to be stripped away.

Can I still trust God? Even if He lets the most terrible thing happen to me? I know He is easily big enough to take care of me so that not one thing will harm me. But . . . but . . . what if it's His will that I suffer? Am *I* willing? Is He big enough to take care of me even through suffering?

I think of all those people whose stories are recounted in *Martyrs Mirror*. I think of the people who are talked about in Hebrews 11. God has plans and purposes that are too big and high for us. YES, He is big enough! I trust my future to Him. Yes, even if the most terrible things happen to me, His grace will be sufficient. His love will be enough.

Romans 8:35, "Who shall separate us from the love of Christ? shall tribulation, or distress . . .?" No. Never!

He Is Able to Deliver.
But if Not . . .

READ: Daniel 3:13-30

Last night at dusk Dina came to sleep here because my husband was gone. Two men came.

"Verton here?"

"No."

"Where is he?"

"On the road."

They came in uninvited. They had hard faces. Tattooed arms.

"I want to buy a handmill."

I went to the storeroom to get one. He followed me inside and began to shine his flashlight along the gap where wall met thatch roof. His evil presence felt too close in the dark.

"Well!" I declared. "I didn't say you could come in here. Is this your house?" He backed off. After much fiddling, he bought the mill and left. I turned to Dina.

"Do we want to sleep here alone tonight?"

"No. I 'fraid. Those same men tried to break in before, when you weren't home." So Dina's parents joined us for the night. I closed up the house. The padlock was gone. I had seen something flash in his hand. My trembling hand toiled long to close the

337

substitute lock. I slept with tension and scary dreams.

Do they want women or money? I prodded my sleepy brain. *What would I do if—?* My strategies for escape were wild. They frightened me more.

"I will trust and not be afraid." I am afraid. Am I not trusting? "Fear not." I want to obey, but how?

Call on the name of Jesus, the blood of Jesus. It has power. By the fear of the Lord men depart from evil, so pray aloud. *Is that a guarantee I'll be unharmed? What about those who have been raped or robbed? Didn't they pray right?*

Perfect love casts out fear. God gave us fear to protect our purity, our life. God gave it. He wants to control it. *God, here is my fear. You delivered the Hebrew three from the fiery furnace. Can You deliver me from fear of the furnace?*

"He heard me, and delivered me from all my fears" (Psalm 34:4).

P.S. It wasn't quite as easy as it sounds. Nancy Stutzman and Martha Barkman gave me the advice that I wrote here. I had to pray much over it until the peace of God controlled my heart and mind again.

Angels Versus Robbers

READ: II Kings 6:13-17

"More money!" demanded the armed robbers. "Give us more dollars. Quickly! We're about to break down the door."

"We've already given you all we have."

"Fast! Get into your car and take us to the new highway."

Eli refused. One jumped into the van, but he didn't get far. It crashed into the chicken house.

Kneeling together, we and our five children continued to plead for God's protection. Had the men left? Would they return? Were they really guerrillas? Were there actually ten, as they had claimed?

Fifteen-year-old Philip prayed, "Thank You, God, that there are more with us than there are with them."

How comforting! What did it matter how many there were? What difference does it make whether two or ten or a thousand men point guns at us? "If God be for us, who can be against us?" (Romans 8:31).

Horses and chariots of fire surrounded Elisha. Our God is the same One who sent the heavenly hosts to defend His prophet. He is with us and protects us, too.

"The angel of the Lord encampeth round about them that fear him, and delivereth them" (Psalm 34:7).

Praise His Name!

God's Power Over Bullets

READ: Isaiah 43:1-5

The pickup stopped short. But it was too late. Shots pierced the night. Thirteen-year-old Ernest saw flashes of fire erupting from automatic rifles. Doubling over on the seat, he shouted, "What is it, John?"

"Salvadorean soldiers," John answered. "They're shooting at us."

Ernest slipped onto the floor as bullets pierced the windshield. Suddenly, a sharp pain seared his buttocks. He had been hit by bullet fragments.

At last! Silence. Soldiers emerged from the darkness and advanced cautiously, their rifles aimed at the suspected vehicle.

"Hands up!" barked the commander. "Everybody out! Lie facedown on the road with your hands behind your heads."

All ten passengers flopped onto the road, amazed that they were actually alive.

"Who's the driver?" demanded the officer. "Get up! Identify yourself. Why didn't you stop at our signal?"

"I didn't see you in the darkness, Sir."

"Where are you coming from? Where are you going?"

"We're returning from distributing food and clothing to flood victims, Sir."

Realizing that they had shot at harmless relief workers, the soldiers became concerned. "Is anyone hurt?" they asked.

"I am," Ernest said. Then he fainted.

Alarmed, the soldiers rushed Ernest to the hospital Surgeons removed the shrapnel and discharged him

Meanwhile, Eli and I awaited our son's return.

"What could've happened, Eli?" I asked my husband. "Where could they be?"

As usual, my husband offered the words I had become so used to hearing, "Trust God. All we can do is trust God and pray."

Trust God? I wanted to! I tried to! But I was finding it so hard to do.

Then, finally, they were home. I felt faint when I saw the riddled pickup. We couldn't understand it. A battalion of soldiers had shot at ten people at close range without killing anyone. It was a miracle!

But a greater miracle took place inside of me. My fearfulness was replaced with assurance. I began to understand something about God's power over bullets. I know now that even in El Salvador, I can trust my heavenly Father

Will It Be Today?

READ: Mark 13:24-27

Today the state milk inspector came. In our state, in order to sell grade-A milk an inspector comes twice a year to make sure the conditions are actually grade-A.

Although we sell grade-A every day and try to keep the conditions as such, when the six months is almost up, we put in extra effort to keep the spiderwebs swept away and the corners clean. Every morning as I give the floor its final hosing I think, "This may be the day." I give the whole milkhouse a critical once-over just to be sure it will pass inspection.

As I walk to the house, I am reminded that this could also be the day of a greater inspection, one that matters much more than a grade-A license. Quickly I check the corners of my mind to see if I have allowed the dust and webs of "things" to accumulate there, crowding out my devotion to God. I examine the load I am carrying to make sure I am not bearing any extra burdens of grudges or fear and anxiety. Am I ready for that great day? Have I claimed the Holy Spirit's presence as oil in my lamp to guide my feet on the path I must tread today?

In this inspection there will be no second chance. I must be ready on the initial appearance of the great Judge of all ages. No excuse will be good enough and time will be ended. Even so, come Lord Jesus!

Ready and Waiting

READ: Matthew 24:42-46; 25:13

My mother called to inform me that we were going to have company on Wednesday. She didn't know whether the folks were planning to surprise me, but, knowing how a place can look with little children, she thought I would like to be prepared. I was glad for the forewarning because I certainly would have been caught off guard.

The house was clean and a roast was in the oven for dinner the day the guests were to arrive. Meanwhile, I kept my ear cocked for the phone call. . . . It never came. The company didn't either!

I called my mother and was told that the guests had decided on a different day.

That later day dawned. Expecting the guests to come about two, I took it easy, thinking that I had plenty of time to tidy my house before their arrival. They arrived at eleven!

Then I thought of our Lord's second coming. We all know He is coming . . . but when? It could be today. Maybe tomorrow or not for several more years. We need to keep our spiritual houses in order and be ready for His arrival at all times, lest we be caught off guard.

BIOGRAPHICAL SKETCHES

Barkman, Martha Stoltzfus (Mrs. Ervin) is a native of Lancaster, Pennsylvania. She served as a Christian day school teacher for five years, with three years in the States and two years in Belize, Central America. She and Ervin were married in 1981 and are the parents of three daughters, Clarita, Jana, and Ervina. In 1983 the couple was sent by Amish Mennonite Aid to Belize to serve in a remote jungle village, accessible only by travel in a dugout on 50 miles of sea and river, or a day's walk on jungle trails. Constant physical dangers kept them trusting continually in the Lord's presence and protection. They have made their home in Lancaster again since their return from Belize in 1987.

Birky, Joanna Hofer (Mrs. Delbert) was born in Alberta, Canada and lived there until her marriage in 1977 to Delbert, a school teacher from Oregon. Delbert was ordained as a minister at Harrisburg, Oregon, a year after their marriage. During the next four years the couple served a term at Maranatha Winter Bible School for youth and cared for foster children. In 1982 they were asked by the Western Conservative Fellowship churches to serve as missionaries in Dangriga, Belize, Central America, where they have lived since. Childlessness, a difficult situation to accept, has made them very grateful for the children God has given them through adoption: Joseph, James and Joyce.

345

Bontrager, Rose Mary Miller (Mrs. Jason) now of San Lucas, Belize, grew up in Iowa and taught in Christian day schools in Ohio, Iowa and Belize. While serving in Belize under Caribbean Light and Truth she met Jason who had volunteered as a carpenter and mechanic. In 1985 they were married and returned to Belize. Since their return they have been blessed with two children, Lois Ann and Joseph. Six weeks after their first colic baby was born Rosy suffered a stroke. Physical recovery from the stroke was more rapid and easy than the mental and emotional healing. Victory over depression was a difficult struggle but healing continues. Rosy has accepted the challenge of editing a monthly Sunday School paper in Kekchi which contains articles for men, women and children.

Byler, Clara Gingerich (Mrs. Nolan) resides near Mt. Eaton, Ohio with her husband who is both minister and physician. They have four children, Shannon, Darren, Sonya and Dustan. Clara says being a doctor and minister's wife presents a continual challenge in acceptance. Opportunities to learn submission, patience and true servanthood are many. She grew up in Kalona, Iowa, where she also taught two years in a Christian day school. When she and Nolan were married in 1978 they moved to Ohio where he began his practice as a physician. Nolan was ordained in 1986. Clara frequently teaches adult women's Sunday School classes.

Glick, Mary June Lapp (Mrs. Melvin) is married to a pastor-farmer and lives in Dundee, New York. She grew up on a farm in Lancaster, Pennsylvania. Her husband was ordained to the ministry in Belize, Central America where the couple served as missionaries for ten years under Amish Mennonite Aid. Myron and Michael were born in Pennsylvania before they went to Belize and while there they adopted Melanie and Mauricio. They returned to Pennsylvania after their term of service and two years later moved to New York. Frequent bouts with sickness, numerous cultural changes, and the shocking suddenness of her mother's death while she was in Belize have served as stepping stones to make Mary June sensitive to the needs of others. Teaching Sunday School and sewing classes has helped her minister to some of those needs.

 Glick, Verda J. Kauffman (Mrs. Eli) a missionary in El Salvador since her marriage to Eli in 1966, was born and brought up in Lancaster, Pennsylvania. Before marriage she worked as an intensive care unit nurse and taught Christian day school, both in Pennsylvania. Teaching experience continues as she home schools their five children, Ernest, Philip, Timothy, Paul and Karen. Along with her calling to be a minister's wife (Eli was ordained in 1973) Verda has served at various times as Sunday School and Women's Bible Class teacher, childbirth preparation and health and hygiene teacher, and instructor of sewing classes. She has also been involved in literacy work and nursing. "My most difficult times were when other missionaries evacuated and war broke out just before Paul was born, and in 1989 when armed robbers came to the house four times," Verda says.

Herschberger, Esther Hochstetler (Mrs. David) grew up on a farm in Goshen, Indiana. She served in Mississippi doing housework in a missionary home, in Arkansas as a cook in a nursing home, and in Red Lake, Ontario, Canada, doing domestic work in the school and in homes. Marriage to David in 1959 changed her location to Arkansas and later to Kitchener, then Hudson, Ontario, where they live presently. Jason, Rhoda, and Philip were born to the couple before David's ordination in 1967. Linford and Lowell have joined the family since. Besides being a missionary pastor, David also manages a bookstore. Esther, from childhood lived with the knowledge that her mother could pass away suddenly from heart failure. Travelling from Hudson, Esther reached her mother's side two hours after she had passed away. Though tempted to be bitter she has experienced the Lord's healing. Teaching Sunday School, conducting Bible studies, and helping part time in their Christian day school are among the responsibilities she has shouldered outside her home.

Martin, Susan Kim Glenn (Mrs. Vernon) spent her childhood years in Lancaster, Ohio, and Logan, Ohio. From 1977 to 1982 she taught school in Virginia and Maryland and helped in the print shop at Christian Light Publications in Virginia. She and Vernon were married in 1981. From 1984-1987 they served under Conservative Mennonite Fellowship Mission in Palama, Guatemala, where two of their children, Benjamin and Marvin where born. Their daughters, Susana and Kendra were born in Maryland. After two years on a Maryland dairy farm, the Martins returned to Guatemala in November, 1989, to serve under Mennonite Air Missions in Novillero. Although he is not ordained, Vernon shares preaching responsibilities on the mission field. Kim says a hospital stay in Guatemala due to a miscarriage combined with news of her husband's imprisonment due to a traffic accident was a time of growth in trusting the Lord.

Miller, Rebecca Anne Martin (Mrs. Verton) claims Ontario, Canada, as her homeland. While working as a rural clinic nurse in El Chal, Guatemala under Mennonite Air Missions she faced the fear of death nightly at the height of Guatemala's guerrilla warfare. Working through the many "whys" of missionary John Troyer's death at the hands of guerrillas was a preparation for later experiences. In 1985 she and Verton were married and two years later were blessed by the birth of a son, Jonathan. They grieved when the Lord took him Home only a month later. Elizabeth June was welcomed into their home in 1989. Since their marriage they have made their home in Columbia Village, Belize, Central America, where Verton serves as lay leader under Caribbean Light and Truth Mission. Villagers are thankful for Anne's nursing and midwifery abilities.

Nisly, Brenda Stoltzfus (Mrs. J. Samuel) left her birthplace and childhood home, Lancaster, Pennsylvania, to serve as cook and kitchen helper in Hillcrest Home, Arkansas, for over a year. Marriage to Sam in 1978 changed her location again to Bird-in-Hand, Pennsylvania, where RoseMary was born. In 1981 they moved to Sam's home area, Partridge, Kansas. Rhoda joined her sister RoseMary there. Amish Mennonite Aid asked the couple to go to Hattieville, Belize, Central America, and they answered the call, serving as missionaries from 1983-1987. Brenda was in charge of women's sewing circle along with caring for her children, J. Mark and J. Luke, also being born during these years. Fearful experiences of robbery in Hattieville brought Brenda to a place of brokenness and a realization that God is her total security. Upon terminating in Belize the family returned to Partridge and have since welcomed Virgil Jon into the family circle.

Stutzman, Nancy Miller (Mrs. David) taught school one year in Mississippi then returned to her home town, Wellman, Iowa, where she married David in 1973. The following year they were sent by Caribbean Light and Truth as missionaries to teach among the Indians at Punta Gorda in southern Belize. Belize was home to their children Regina, Nathan, Konrad (died at age 6), Jonathan, LouAnn and Marsha until the family moved to Iowa in 1989. Facing pioneer jungle life, having singles live in with their family for years, and living through and accepting the sudden death of their son (through a tractor accident) have been hard times for Nancy. God has used them to make her more readily aware of and caring about the hurts and needs of others.

Weaver, Jo Ellen Skrivseth (Mrs. John) was born and grew up in northern Minnesota. In 1968 she taught eight weeks of Summer Bible School in Kentucky, then went to help her older sister in British Columbia for a year. In 1969 she married John. The couple lived in Zanesville, Ohio, for two years until they moved to Wisconsin where John was ordained in 1976. They, with their five children, Mark, Daniel, Delvin, Kristina and Lovina, live on a dairy farm. The Lord has sent trials to Jo Ellen through physical ailments which brought emotional stresses as well. These experiences have taught her of woman's frailty and her ultimate Source of Strength.

Each entry is identified by the writer's teacup.

This cup will mark the three entries submitted anonymously.

350

Christian Light Publications, Inc., is a nonprofit conservative Mennonite publishing company providing Christ-centered, Biblical literature in a variety of forms including Gospel tracts, books, Sunday school materials, summer Bible school materials, and a full curriculum for Christian day schools and home schools.

For more information at no obligation or for spiritual help, please write to us at:

Christian Light Publications, Inc.
P. O. Box 1212
Harrisonburg, VA 22801-1212